RESCUE OF
THE BOUNTY

RESCUE OF THE BOUNTY

YOUNG READERS EDITION

Disaster and Survival
in Superstorm Sandy

**MICHAEL J. TOUGIAS
AND DOUGLAS A. CAMPBELL**

HENRY HOLT AND COMPANY

NEW YORK

Henry Holt and Company, *Publishers since 1866*
Henry Holt® is a registered trademark of Macmillan Publishing Group, LLC
120 Broadway, New York, NY 10271 • mackids.com

Our books may be purchased in bulk for promotional, educational, or
business use. Please contact your local bookseller or the Macmillan
Corporate and Premium Sales Department at (800) 221–7945 ext. 5442
or by email at MacmillanSpecialMarkets@macmillan.com.

Library of Congress Cataloging-in-Publication Data is available.

First edition, 2022
Book design by Mallory Grigg
Printed in the United States of America by Bang Printing,
Brainerd, Minnesota

ISBN 978-1-250-83139-2 (hardcover)
10 9 8 7 6 5 4 3 2 1

To the BOUNTY *crew and*
Catalina and Vanessa Smith

CONTENTS

PART I

PART II

PART III

TRUE RESCUE
RESCUE OF
THE BOUNTY

PART I

CHAPTER 1

The Speech

The autumn afternoon was perfect on the New London, Connecticut, waterfront. The rippled river water sparkled; the blue above as clear as freshly washed laundry.

At the dock, a ship named *Bounty*, with three towering masts and a black hull, floated serenely in the sunshine. Standing on the ship's deck was its captain, Robin Walbridge, a quiet, confident man. Although the captain was relaxed, the day had been fraught with more than a little tension.

The fifteen crew members who served under the captain had received anxious text messages or phone calls from family and friends. They knew the 180-foot,

50-year-old wooden ship—an expanded replica of the original, famous 1784 *Bounty* from England—was going to sail south to Florida.

They also knew that a hurricane was brewing in the Bahamas and heading north.

A twenty-five-year-old crewman, Joshua Scornavacchi, had received a text message from his mother in Pennsylvania. She was worried about a hurricane named Sandy. "I'll be fine," he replied, adding that *Bounty* had been through rough weather before.

But other crew members were quite concerned. They had heard that the hurricane had the potential to grow into a monster storm.

The first mate, John Svendsen, forty-one, now in his third season aboard *Bounty*, had talked earlier in the day with his junior officers. The conversation convinced Svendsen, who had his own misgivings, that he needed to talk with Captain Walbridge. He knew the captain planned to start sailing south that evening despite the oncoming storm. Svendsen wanted to present the captain with options.

Svendsen thought *Bounty* should stay in New London or perhaps sail north to protected harbors such as New Bedford or Boston. In fact, sailing toward Bermuda, 650 miles to the southeast, might be an option. Almost any direction was better than going due south to Florida.

In addition, Svendsen and some of the other crew members became aware of a problem with the *Bounty's* pumps when they were washing the deck that morning.

There were two hoses, neatly stowed on deck, one to reach forward to the bow, the other that extended to the stern. On the ship's third and lowest deck, down a set of stairs and then a ladder, there were two diesel engines. The engines powered electrical generators. Those generators ran the pumps set in the bottom-most part of the ship, called the bilge, that sucked the water out. Ocean water that seeped into the vessel through tiny gaps in its wooden planking collected in the bilge. Without pumps, *Bounty* would eventually sink, like any leaky wooden boat.

There were pipes and hoses extending from the two pumps to the bilge space below the floorboards of the third deck. Any water that collected in that bilge space was sucked through the hoses and pipes and discharged back into the sea. But the process could be reversed, with seawater sucked up into the deck-washing hoses.

It was this seawater that the team was using to clean the decks that bright autumn morning. One team member noticed something different, troubling. Instead of a powerful stream, the washdown hoses were giving him barely enough spray to wet the deck boards. That meant that the pumps didn't have the proper power. So if water was coming into the ship in bad weather, the pumps wouldn't suck it out fast enough or at the proper strength. He mentioned the problem to his two teammates, who seemed unfazed. Then the worried crewman reported his concerns to the ship's engineer. In the end, the pump problem was ignored.

First Mate Svendsen put that problem aside—his focus was on the hurricane—until he finally had a chance to talk to Captain Walbridge alone.

"There are people concerned about the hurricane," Svendsen told his boss. "I want to discuss options, including staying here."

Walbridge listened to his first mate, as he always did, and then he offered his own thoughts. He said he would hold a meeting with the crew and explain his plan.

Walbridge conducted an all-hands meeting at about five o'clock. Often, Walbridge used these meetings as teaching opportunities, since he saw his purpose aboard *Bounty* in part as an educator. In fact, he had come from a family of teachers, as far back as grandparents and some great-grandparents.

This meeting would be different, though. Walbridge, celebrating his sixty-third birthday that afternoon, climbed atop a small deckhouse called the Navigation (Nav) Shack (an enclosed area with a chart table and navigation and communication equipment) and, in his quiet way, began talking.

On this afternoon, he had already come to a decision and selected a path for the ship to travel. Certainly there were alternative routes for *Bounty* in the days to come. Like the chess player he'd been for fifty-five years, the captain had considered all those moves and dismissed them.

"There is a hurricane headed this way," he told his fifteen shipmates, the falling sun at his back. "It's called Frankenstorm. There will be sixty-knot winds and rough seas. The boat's safer being out at sea than being buckled up at a dock somewhere." Then he laughed a little and, as if in jest, added: "You guys will probably be safer if you take a train inland." The levity ended there.

"If anyone wants to go ashore, now is the time. I won't think any less of you. Come back to *Bounty* when the weather clears up."

No one budged, nor did anyone speak.

"My plan is to sail south by east, to take some time and

see what the storm is going to do." He told them about hurricanes *Bounty* had encountered under his command. The ship had made it through then, and she would do so now.

Still, no one spoke. First Mate Svendsen, who had given his captain his best advice, did not share his earlier concerns. He now accepted the Walbridge plan as prudent.

Nor did the second and third mates or the bosun give voice to their doubts.

Some of the crew members were nervous as they looked up at Walbridge. Some were excited for a new adventure after a summer of largely tranquil voyages. The moment for objections passed. Everyone—even the new cook, who had first boarded *Bounty* the night before—went to work, preparing to set sail.

The sun had slipped behind the railroad terminal just inshore from the city dock, and Dockmaster Barbara Neff saw that *Bounty* was leaving. She stood for a moment and enjoyed the spectacle: a vessel of ancient proportions departing into the gathering dusk, heading south toward a monster storm.

CHAPTER 2

Heading to the Open Ocean

THURSDAY EVENING, OCTOBER 25

Bounty has departed New London, CT . . . Next Port of Call . . .
St. Petersburg, Florida.

Bounty will be sailing due East out to sea before heading
South to avoid the brunt of Hurricane Sandy.

Entry on *HMS Bounty* Facebook page,

6:06 p.m., October 25, 2012

Adam Prokosh had been aboard *Bounty* for most of the
last eight months. On the evening of October 25, he
watched as the ship passed the redbrick Ledge Light-
house and entered the Long Island Sound off the

Connecticut coast. Prokosh, twenty-seven, of Seattle, had spent several years on a number of tall ships before he joined the crew of the *Bounty*. He had been impressed with much of what he found aboard the old ship that, at times, was referred to by detractors as a "movie prop."

True, *Bounty* had been built in 1960 in Lunenburg, Nova Scotia, for use in the movie *Mutiny on the Bounty*, starring Marlon Brando. More recently, it had played a role in two Pirates of the Caribbean movies.

But the ship's architect had created a rugged vessel. MGM Studios actually sailed the *Bounty* all the way to Tahiti. While serving as a movie set, the ship also doubled as the base of operations for the film crew and actors. The tall ship was an expanded version of the original *HMS Bounty*, which became infamous when the crew of that British ship mutinied in 1789 in the South Pacific. The mutineers took over the ship and put captain William Bligh and his remaining followers in a small open boat to fend for themselves. The ship made for the movie was larger than the original, with a 120-foot hull at the waterline. Inside were diesel-powered generators, air conditioning, and other amenities necessary for moviemaking in the tropics.

Prokosh had heard stories about the ship's adventures

under Robin Walbridge and believed *Bounty* to be fundamentally seaworthy. And he was impressed equally by the way the crew was organized and informed. Communications aboard *Bounty*, Prokosh felt, were better than on any of the other vessels he'd sailed. When he heard about sailing toward Hurricane Sandy, he was excited.

"Sailing is a sport and a team sport," he would tell people. "This is the big game. End of the season. This is what we train for."

Earlier in the day, Prokosh had gone into a New London bar, where a patron who recognized him as a member of *Bounty*'s crew accosted him.

At that point, Prokosh knew few details about the approaching hurricane.

"You guys will be crazy leaving the dock," the bar patron told Prokosh.

"Are you kidding me?" he replied. "This is going to be great weather!"

The open ocean came into view around midnight as *Bounty* approached the flashing white light on a tower at the end of Montauk Point, Long Island. At that time, the four members of the next watch came on duty to guide the ship. They found the seas calm and the skies clear as they assumed watch duties. For an hour at a time, each watch stander steered *Bounty* by its big wooden steering wheel, called the helm (just aft of the rear—or mizzen— mast). They also stood watch for an hour near the bow, where they were responsible for spotting traffic or obstacles.

In the six hours since leaving the dock, all of *Bounty*'s crew members had been on duty. Walbridge told the new cook, Jessica Black, thirty-four, to hold off on the evening meal so that all hands could focus on running the ship and putting gear in its proper place. She put the chili she had prepared on simmer in the galley at the forward end of the middle—or "tween"—deck and pitched in with the other crew members.

Everyone was engaged in "sea stowing," a practice of securing everything on and below deck so that nothing could be dislodged in the event of violent rocking of the ship during foul weather.

Walbridge had trained the crew to have the storm sails—smaller than sails used in moderate weather—ready in the case of rising winds. Prokosh oversaw that work.

When all was done and dark had settled over *Bounty*, the crew went down to the tween deck and then forward to the galley, where the steaming chili awaited them. Perhaps it was the hard work that primed their appetites, but all aboard felt the new cook had exceeded their expectations.

During the meal, the A-watch was on duty—their hours were always from 8:00 a.m. to noon or 8:00 p.m. to midnight. First Mate John Svendsen was the watch captain. He was distinguishable aboard *Bounty* by his shoulder-length, smoothly groomed brown hair. The Minnesota native was articulate and measured. Svendsen was aware that aboard a tall ship, there was much to learn. He said at one point he looked for mentors to help him grow in the maritime industry. Aboard *Bounty*, he was second-in-command. Only Robin Walbridge stood above him, and there was talk that, when Walbridge retired in three years, Svendsen would replace him.

Also on the A-watch was Claudene Christian, age forty-two. Originally from Alaska, Christian was a former Miss Teen Alaska. She was outgoing with a "bubbly" personality.

Christian claimed to be a distant relative of Fletcher Christian, the master's mate aboard the original *HMS Bounty*. In Tahiti in April 1789, Fletcher Christian led a mutiny and seized control of the ship from Captain William Bligh.

After moving on from a failed business venture, Christian returned to live with her parents in Oklahoma. But

Christian was soon bored in Oklahoma and wanted a new start in life. She was single and over forty, and her life was at a dead end. Then in May, with no significant tall-ship experience, she joined *Bounty*'s crew as a volunteer and loved life aboard the ship. For the first time in a long, long time, she felt at peace and happy.

One of the reasons Christian stayed on board *Bounty* when it left New London was that she was dating the ship's second mate, Matt Sanders. And Christian said she wanted to see the voyage through.

Family members had tried to convince Christian to go ashore. She replied: "*Bounty* loves hurricanes, haven't you heard? The Captain has thirty years' experience. All will be ok. We will go as far east has we can. We may be halfway to Europe to get around it."

Once *Bounty* was underway, but before the ship was far out to sea, Christian looked up more information about the hurricane on her phone. When she saw fellow crew member Jessica Hewitt, she repeated her earlier thought. "The storm looks like it will be so enormous, we are going to have to go halfway to Europe."

Then she called her mother. Dina Christian was busy at that moment and asked if she could call back, but her daughter sounded frantic.

"No! We are out on the ocean, and I'm afraid I'm going to lose reception. I gotta tell you how much I love you. I really do." A little later, there was a text message on Dina Christian's phone. "If I go down with the ship and the worst happens, just know that I AM TRULY, GENUINELY HAPPY."

Did Christian have a premonition? Or was it just her intuition telling her that Captain Walbridge was not taking the storm seriously enough? No matter the process by which her doubts arose, her sense of trepidation was real, and it was well-founded.

If he was going to be heading toward a hurricane, Prokosh was pleased to be sailing with a crew he respected. Yes, with only sixteen aboard, *Bounty* had her smallest crew since leaving San Juan in April. *But these sixteen*, Prokosh thought, *are the right ones. They know the boat well, and they really will give you their best.*

CHAPTER 3

The Captain

FRIDAY MORNING, OCTOBER 26

This will be a tough voyage for Bounty. Here is Bounty's current position and the weather front (Hurricane Sandy) that is approaching.

Bounty is 100 miles off shore. Speed 8.6 knots on a course South by west.

Entry on *HMS Bounty* Facebook page,

9:45 a.m., October 26, 2012

At about 8:00 a.m. on Friday morning, around the time Hurricane Sandy was hammering the Abacos Islands one hundred miles or more off the Florida coast, the officers of *Bounty* gathered. They met on the stern of the tween deck in what was called the Great Cabin. Eating breakfast while they talked, Walbridge, First Mate Svendsen, Second Mate Sanders, Third Mate Dan Cleveland, Bosun Laura Groves, and Engineer Chris Barksdale discussed the weather. The forecasts they were getting by email and radio continued to predict that the path of the hurricane would bring it directly toward *Bounty*.

They talked about work that would be performed that day by *Bounty*'s crew. A yard—the horizontal wooden spar that holds the top of a square sail—would be lowered to the deck to reduce weight aloft. And there was more sea stowing to be performed so that when the seas grew and the ship rocked, there would be no loose items to become projectiles, flying across the ship's thirty-one-foot beam and threatening the crew.

The officers also talked about the navigation plans. At the moment, the engines were running hard—uncommon aboard *Bounty*. Usually, when the ship lost sight of land, the captain, for authenticity and as a means of teaching, turned off most mechanical equipment and reverted to practices used in the days of sail. But today Captain Walbridge wanted to cover as many miles as possible toward Florida while the seas were still calm.

Once the officers' meeting was concluded, it was time

for the daily Captain's Muster (meeting), when the entire crew gathered around the captain.

Muster was the one time in any normal day when all the crew saw Walbridge, a time when the skipper might tell a joke or two, and when, invariably, he would use the opportunity to teach his young crewmates something new about seamanship. The crew had deep respect for the captain and looked forward to these sessions when he would share his knowledge.

At least superficially, this explains why no one had left *Bounty* back in New London. If they stayed aboard long enough, as Third Mate Dan Cleveland had, a crew member learned to trust what the captain said.

Among his fifteen crew members—ten men and five women—aboard for this voyage, Walbridge had unquestioning loyalty.

Douglas Faunt, sixty-six, of Oakland, California, was the oldest crew member, three years older than Walbridge. A wealthy electronics expert who had built and sold a company to provide the funds for world traveling, Faunt had sailed aboard *Bounty* as a volunteer off and on since 2005. His feelings were typical. If asked, he would tell you he loved Walbridge, found him a person who others could emulate, a person who was going to teach everything he knew.

Although there always seemed to be eager applicants for crew positions, not every sailor who stepped aboard *Bounty* shared Faunt's belief in the skipper when they returned ashore.

It was late in November 2010 when Andrew Seguin got a call telling him that *Bounty* was looking for crew for a voyage to Puerto Rico, leaving Boothbay Harbor, Maine, the next day.

Seguin called Marc Castells, a college friend who had lost his job and told him about *Bounty*.

"You have twenty-four hours if you want to do this," he told Castells.

"The only information I had before getting on the boat was that it was leaving Maine and was ending up in Puerto Rico," Seguin said. "We drove through the night to get there and literally pulled into Boothbay Harbor when the sun was coming up." It was November 27, past the end of the hurricane season.

Seguin had never sailed on a tall ship.

"We ended up leaving Boothbay under motor," Seguin said. "It was gorgeous. It was cold. There were dolphins jumping off the bow." As *Bounty* headed south, the friends spent the first couple of days getting used to the routine of the ship.

On the first morning, Walbridge told the crew he didn't worry about fire on the boat because it was old and wet. He was also unconcerned about sinking. "He said he'd had many engineers who said the boat has enough buoyancy in itself that it won't sink," Seguin recalled.

"One thing that he emphasized," Seguin added, "was that 'man overboard' was the most dangerous thing on the boat. The boat can't sail into the wind." This meant that if any of the crew were to fall into the water, they would be quickly left behind, as the ship would struggle to turn around to rescue the crew member.

"We did overboard drills almost every day," Castells recalled. The drill involved lowering a small rowboat called a dinghy overboard and using it to pick up an object thrown into the water in place of an actual man-overboard.

As the weather worsened, Walbridge told the crew that in these conditions, *Bounty* could not even be turned around. For those cases, there was a drum at the stern, packed with safety and survival gear and an electronic device that could notify coast guard search-and-rescue units.

Everyone on board was taught that if they fell overboard, they could find the big drum floating in *Bounty*'s wake.

Later the wind rose, hitting thirty knots. The crew started to see sails tearing and blowing out. Seguin, a conservative sailor, went to Walbridge and questioned the amount of sail *Bounty* was flying.

"Robin told me: 'I've gone through hurricanes with three of them up,'" Seguin said. "That's when I was, like, Okay, I don't like this situation, but I'm not in control, so I do what I'm told."

Then another sail blew out and eight hands were sent aloft. Castells followed First Mate John Svendsen—in his first year aboard *Bounty* and his first year aboard a square-rigged ship—up the rope ladder called a ratline. *Bounty* rolled 30 degrees to each side, driven by gale-force winds that blew up the shredded sections of the torn sail into canvas balloons.

And then the topmast broke and folded over its lower half.

Seguin had stayed on deck. At first, he saw the back-stays, ropes which hold the masts up and keep them from falling forward, sagging. Then he saw the mast break above where Castells was working.

And then the weather got worse. *Bounty* was headed dead center into the storm.

Meanwhile, *Bounty*'s bilges were filling with water.

Seguin learned that boards in the bilge meant to keep seawater near the pumps had been removed when they rotted. On the violently rocking ship, the pumps didn't work.

"Once we got into the thick of the storm, I don't know how far we were rolling, but it was huge," Seguin explained. "There's stuff all over the floor. At the same time, the timbers of the boat worked endlessly in bone-crunching moaning, creaking [so loud] that you pretty much have to yell, not over the motors but over the boat."

As a general observation, Seguin noted that Walbridge stayed in his cabin except when he gave his morning talk. He ran the boat by delegation. His first mate, John Svendsen, had as recently as two years earlier been employed as a dive boat captain in Hawaii, not the sort of credentials Sequin expected of the person second-in-command of a massive, tall ship.

As *Bounty* neared Bermuda, with the bilge pumps overwhelmed, Seguin said he came up behind Walbridge, who was writing an email to home base. In it, Seguin said,

Walbridge wrote that things were not going so well and asked that parts be sent overnight to Bermuda.

"This is not what he's telling everyone [in the crew]," Seguin said.

Bounty did dock in Bermuda, and Seguin and Castells informed Walbridge they were leaving. The skipper was pleasant when he accepted their resignations. New job applicants ashore were told that the two friends had left because they were seasick.

CHAPTER 4

Preparations for the Storm

Friday was a good day at sea. The winds were moderate, the seas relatively calm as *Bounty*'s bow plowed south across the Atlantic. Long Island, New York, had disappeared in her wake. Now, there was dark blue water in every direction, with only thin lines of foam atop small waves. The crew knew change was coming, though. They had their weather fax, which transmitted information to them about the weather and climate conditions, among other modern conveniences, to remind them that Sandy was headed north. So those sailors not on watch began tackling the jobs on Bosun Laura Groves's list.

The C-watch, Joshua Scornavacchi's crew, finished its last tour at eight o'clock, ate breakfast, and now was available to help Groves. There were safety ropes called jack lines to be strung along the top—or weather—deck and on the wide-open sections of the tween deck just below. Jack lines are a safety item aboard sailing vessels; their purpose in rough seas is to give crew members a place on deck either to hold on or to clip onto with a tether attached to a harness to stop them from falling and sliding overboard.

There was "sailor-strainer" netting to be raised along the exposed sides of the weather deck, which would keep a crew member from falling into the sea.

Scornavacchi, as nimble as any of the crew members, was sent aloft to reef some of the sails, a normal tactic prior to foul weather and rising winds. Reefing is the process of gathering up part of a sail into folds, thus reducing the area of sail exposed to the wind.

Scornavacchi loved the outdoors and adventure. He had earned his Eagle rank in the Boy Scouts and had the grades to attend Penn State University after high school. It was there that his passion for the outdoors really soared.

He went camping, backpacking, rock climbing, and

scuba diving. In the summer, he worked as a white-water-rafting and kayaking guide in nearby Jim Thorpe, Pennsylvania.

Scornavacchi lived to hike in the snow. In this and other activities, he was alone, which pleased him.

There was a ten-inch snow cover in the forest one February day when, alone, he headed into the woods. Reaching a campsite, he set up his tent and spent the night. The following morning, he was headed out of the woods with a sixty-pound pack on his back when his knee snapped, tearing his meniscus. His leg was stuck in one spot.

Still, he made it out of the woods undeterred.

Later, he would go back for more. Perhaps he was testing himself. He wanted the whole experience and believed if he held back, he would only get part of it. If danger and pain were part of the event, he accepted that.

Now, *Bounty* was part of the experience.

Twenty-four hours into her voyage and nearing sunset, *Bounty* made seven knots across the Atlantic Ocean, and was due east from Atlantic City, New Jersey. The seas had been between three and four feet, the wind ranging from ten to fifteen knots, but by now, everything on board

Bounty was lashed in place, prepared for the coming storm. The big diesel engines thrummed two decks below the helm, propelling the ship south.

But by midnight as Friday gave way to Saturday, the waves were eight to twelve feet, and the wind was touching twenty-five knots. The ship handled the building seas well, and the wind allowed the crew to raise some of the sails to augment the engine power. Sailing was what the crew loved, and their spirits were high. They knew that in the hours to come the weather would deteriorate, but they had confidence in Captain Walbridge and counted on him to determine a course that would bypass the strongest part of the approaching hurricane.

And in the Nav Shack, the barometer had begun to fall. The barometer is an instrument that measures atmospheric pressure, and, in general, if the pressure is dropping, it signals bad weather is coming. The *Bounty*'s barometer was now falling in small increments. Steadily. The ship's officers believed when they met at eight o'clock in the morning that Hurricane Sandy was performing as predicted and that Captain Walbridge's plan was still valid: Sail south by east, and then, depending on the latest track of Sandy, make adjustments as needed to stay away from the storm.

There was confidence aboard *Bounty* that all the work

the crew had finished a week before in Boothbay Harbor had put their ship in good stead to face what lay ahead. At Boothbay, the crew and professional carpenters had done their best to caulk between the wooden planks of the hull to slow any leaks. The ship had also suffered some damage to the planks themselves during a hard docking a couple weeks earlier, and that needed to be inspected. It was possible that even the primary structural timbers had been damaged.

Few, if any, of the crew were aware of the emphatic warning Robin Walbridge heard back in the shipyard.

Walbridge told Todd Kosakowski, the boatyard manager and carpenter, about the hard docking and the potential damage. So when the ship was hauled out of the water, Kosakowski was on the lookout for damage.

As the work aboard *Bounty* progressed, Kosakowski focused on the repair of the port quarter where it had struck the dock. His preference was to replace the full length of each plank, but Walbridge wanted a less expensive, though weaker, solution.

On closer inspection of the yard work, Kosakowski thought the planks should have been in better condition. Some had rot and cracks, which had weakened the wood.

Kosakowski told Walbridge the entire boat should be

inspected to see how far the rot went. Then the most severe areas should be dug out and replaced.

Walbridge said the search for widespread rot—a time-consuming and costly project—would have to wait until next year. He assured Kosakowski that he would have the crew paint over the places where rot had been discovered.

Kosakowski informed the skipper that he was more than worried about what he had found under *Bounty*'s exterior. Walbridge replied that he was "terrified," too. Kosakowski later would say that he had urged Walbridge to avoid heavy weather wherever *Bounty* went after leaving the yard.

Before he left Boothbay Harbor, Walbridge relayed to Kosakowski the message he had given to *Bounty*'s owner: "Get rid of the boat as soon as possible."

Walbridge and the boat's owner, a businessman from Long Island, were well aware that the needed repairs could be quite expensive.

CHAPTER 5

A Fateful Change of Course

SATURDAY, OCTOBER 27

Bounty Update . . . Bounty is currently 250 miles due east of the Chesapeake Bay on a Southwest course at 6.8 knots. The Captain reports that Bounty should be encountering weather from the storm sometime this evening.

Entry on *HMS Bounty* Facebook page,

9:44 a.m., October 27

Around noon on Saturday, Captain Walbridge made a fateful decision. He emerged from his cabin and gave the order to change course. *Bounty* had gone far enough to the east and it was time to head southwest.

The skipper told John Svendsen that the latest forecast for the hurricane was for it to continue coming north along the Eastern Seaboard of the United States. It was not going to make landfall in North Carolina, as some meteorologists had said was a possibility. So Walbridge wanted to cut across the top of the hurricane's path. The southwesterly course, he let the crew know through Svendsen, would take the *Bounty* into the storm's northwest quadrant, where the winds should be a bit slower.

The reason for slower winds has to do with the direction a hurricane is traveling and the way in which its winds circle the eye of the storm. A hurricane's winds spin around the eye of the storm in a counterclockwise manner. So the northwest quadrant would be blowing from northeast to south. The winds in this quadrant would be slightly offset because the hurricane itself was traveling in the opposite direction, from south to north. For example, if the winds are sixty knots going south and the storm is traveling at a rate of fifteen knots going north, the fifteen-knot rate of the storm's movement is subtracted from the sixty-knot wind, resulting in wind speed of forty-five knots.

After giving the order to change course, Walbridge

returned to his small office across the tween deck from his cabin. Everyone who sailed aboard *Bounty* knew Walbridge as a traditional captain, one who delegated the hour-by-hour running of his ship to his officers and who otherwise did not mingle with the crew.

This fit Walbridge's personality, his quiet, taciturn nature, his penchant since childhood for keeping his plans—and his life—closed to the outside world. Indeed, his life was so shuttered that even his most trusted subordinates did not know much about his personal life.

Back when he was a long-haul trucker, he invested his money wisely, and at the age of thirty, he retired from trucking and spent more time on the water. He moved from the northeast to Florida, and after earning his captain's license, he then skippered various vessels. In 1994, he took command of *Bounty*.

By 2012, when the hurricane approached, *Bounty* was fifty years old, well beyond middle age in ship years. Walbridge understood the defects of his aging wooden ship. *Bounty* needed constant attention. She was high maintenance. Walbridge knew that, knew that she had her issues. He was aware of the rot in her planking and the limited power of her pumps.

And now, as darkness overcame both the Atlantic and

Saturday, October 27, he was preparing to put those issues to the test.

———————

The seas had built all day and now ran near twenty-five feet, blown by a forty-knot wind. The waves were rolling *Bounty* from side to side, creating a couple of problems new for the ship's 2012 season, if not unique in the ship's fifty-year life.

Having spent the whole season in relatively placid waters, the planking above the waterline was dry, not swollen with water and pressed together. The dryness allowed water to enter *Bounty*'s hull when the ship rolled enough to rock its dry topsides beneath the waves.

More water than usual was boarding *Bounty*. The pumps that were supposed to remove that water were whimpering slackers.

Bosun Laura Groves, in her third year aboard *Bounty*, noticed the pump problem during the day on Saturday. She saw the captain—who seldom strayed from his cabin except for musters—was in the engine room manning the bilge pumps. To Groves, that indicated that *Bounty* had too few crew members. She offered to relieve Walbridge.

What Groves then discovered was that the electric

pumps, attached to a piping system that ran fore and aft to the eight compartments on the lower deck, were weak. They could not hold a "prime." That is, the pumps would start sucking water from the bilge but suddenly suck air instead. Then Groves had to work a series of valves to attempt to restore the suction.

Groves was only the latest crew member to notice the lack of prime in the pumps.

Doug Faunt, on A-watch, had felt there was a problem during the voyage earlier in the week from Boothbay Harbor to New London. When he'd reported his concerns to John Svendsen, the first mate, and to Captain Walbridge, the skipper acknowledged that "Maybe we have some problems." Faunt thought his concerns were taken seriously, but he wasn't certain how seriously. And like most of the other crew members who questioned their own judgment when compared with the skipper's, he didn't pursue the matter.

But now as the wave heights were building, the pumps were losing their prime quite often and not keeping up with the water seeping down into the belly of the ship. Crew members did not find any clogs in the hoses and were unable to fix the problem. The more experienced crew members knew that if the seas kept building and the pumps couldn't keep up with the incoming water, they would be in real danger. That is why Captain Walbridge was taking an active role in trying to solve the problem with the pumps. If they couldn't fix them, the ship would be at the mercy of the storm.

CHAPTER 6

Taking a Beating

SUNDAY MORNING, OCTOBER 28

At Captain Walbridge's command, both engines were running as hard as anyone had ever seen them run. *Bounty* was racing to the southwest, attempting to pass across the projected path of Hurricane Sandy, consuming fuel at an extraordinary rate as the ship's bluff bow banged against the growing seas.

The noise in the engine room was deafening, and it was hot in there.

Claudene Christian was well aware that water was coming in through small openings in the seams in *Bounty*'s side. Little things were happening, and Christian, if she wasn't yet voicing doubt, was becoming concerned.

She likely thought about her decision back in New London to stay on the ship, despite her worries about the hurricane. There was nothing she could do except assist the more experienced crew members with the many tasks they faced as the waves battered *Bounty*.

There was French toast heating in the galley oven when Laura Groves got up on Sunday morning. She helped herself to a serving and then, making her way the length of the tween deck while *Bounty* rocked, slammed, and groaned, she joined her fellow officers for the morning meeting in the Great Cabin at the stern. There was a chart laid out on a table, and the officers took note of their position and that of the hurricane.

Although Sandy was still quite a distance to the southwest, it was clear that at the moment, *Bounty* was crossing directly in front of the approaching storm. It was like crossing railroad tracks and seeing the train coming a mile away. The crossing wasn't a problem if they didn't linger or stall.

It is sound practice if caught at sea with a hurricane to get on the slower side of the storm's winds. Based on *Bounty*'s position and that of the approaching hurricane,

Walbridge calculated that he had time to make it to that favorable left side of Sandy's circulating winds.

He could yet aim for a safe harbor. As the officers met in the Great Cabin, *Bounty* was almost due east of the entrance to the Chesapeake Bay, with the harbors around Norfolk within hours. The ship clearly had issues that could better be addressed in protected waters.

While this crew was working in *Bounty*'s belly, another was up in the rigging. A sail became unfurled and was wildly flapping in the wind. All the deck officers and several of the deckhands—men and women—now scrambled up the rigging.

Everyone made it up to the second yard, where the fore course was whipping and snapping, adding its own racket to the ocean's roar and the wind's howl.

Once at the yard, they stepped away from the mast and, like acrobats on a high wire, onto a single foot rope. There was a back rope behind them, and they each had on a climbing harness that they clipped to the nearest fixed rope.

But now they were face-to-face with the fore course—a large, white spread of fabric that, driven by fifty-knot winds, viciously slapped their faces. At the same time, flailing lines—buntlines used to furl the sail—whipped at the crew. Scornavacchi's arms were cut repeatedly as he struggled with the sail cloth, which ballooned before him, stretched so tight he could not get a grasp. As soon as he got a grip and begin pulling the sail in, the wind would yank it from his grasp.

"Punch it!" yelled John Svendsen, standing on the foot rope beside him.

Scornavacchi punched, the balloon collapsed and he was able to grab a fistful of fabric.

Punching again and again, Scornavacchi over time gathered most of the port side of the sail and had it furled.

While *Bounty*'s crew wrestled with the fore course, Coast Guard Sector North Carolina, in Wilmington, was keeping an eye on Sandy. A year earlier, Hurricane Irene had hit the Outer Banks, and a repeat in 2012 was the biggest concern.

The folks at Sector North Carolina didn't know on Sunday morning that there were any vessels at sea in their neighborhood. What they did know was that Sandy was a massive weather system, a very large hurricane that stretched 800 to 860 miles across.

The district search and rescue (SAR) coordinator, Commander Jimmy Mitchell, had alerted the eight small boat stations along the Outer Banks and the bays. As usual, those units were monitoring marine radios in case there was a vessel in distress.

The coast guard's primary search and rescue "assets" in the mid-Atlantic area—its helicopters and fixed-wing aircraft—were typically stationed at Elizabeth City, North Carolina, just south of the Virginia border. But on Sunday, October 28, the winds had been blowing for a full day too fiercely for the C-130 airplane to take off and land from that airfield. So all the fixed-wing planes had been moved inland, to Raleigh, North Carolina. They could fly from there if necessary. And the coast guard's helicopters—which have a substantially shorter range than the fixed-wing craft—were ordered to remain "on deck" and ready in Elizabeth City.

Bounty's rub rail, its deck level, was getting submerged from time to time in the building seas as the ship heeled 30 degrees to starboard. Moving about the deck—any deck—was a serious challenge. This was the sort of sea and the kind of challenge that Scornavacchi had been looking for when he signed on to *Bounty*, and now, when he wasn't engaged in a chore, he was on the weather deck, filming the chaos and violence there.

The evidence of the storm was belowdecks, too. The port generator and the port engine had stopped running. The starboard generator was working, powering the bilge pumps. But the pumps were increasingly ineffective. On boat check earlier, Scornavacchi had noted both failures, and he reported them to his watch captain, Dan Cleveland.

Meanwhile in the galley, Jessica Black was struggling. The cook attempted to boil water in a pot and the pot flew into a bulkhead. She held her personal jack line with one hand while with the other she cooked hot dogs and macaroni and cheese for lunch for a crew that was exhausted and losing its appetite.

The seas were nearly thirty feet high, the winds gusting close to fifty knots.

About fifteen minutes later, at around eleven o'clock Sunday morning, Robin Walbridge returned to the engine room. Above the roar of the starboard engine and generator, he heard the news from the *Bounty*'s engineer, Chris Barksdale. The ship was taking on even more water than before. The level in the bilge had risen to thirty inches, double what it would normally be.

Walbridge remained silent. He tried to fix the pumps but was unsuccessful and then went back to his office to, presumably, think through his limited options.

Meanwhile, the waves continued to increase. As noon approached, Barksdale had become seasick, nauseated but not vomiting. He could stand the one hundred–degree engine room heat only so long before he needed to breathe fresh air. He was becoming dehydrated. After fifteen minutes, he would have to go topside. But while in the engine room, he saw water flowing in sheets down the inside of the hull—a substantial amount of water. When he saw First Mate Svendsen and Third Mate Cleveland, he mentioned these waterfalls inside *Bounty*'s hull. They wondered whether it was not simply water that had washed up the side of the boat when *Bounty* rolled. "No," Barksdale said. "This water is coming in through the hull."

Barksdale knew it was not only the ship that was taking a beating. He had already wrenched one arm and badly bruised a leg in falls.

Barksdale went to the tween deck for a break and found Walbridge in the Great Cabin. The two men were alone in what might have been the quietest spot aboard *Bounty* when, without warning, the ship lurched, catching Walbridge off guard, catapulting him through the air, backward. A solid table bolted directly to the deck met Walbridge's spine, halting his flight and dropping him to the floor. The table didn't move. Barksdale was amazed that Walbridge did. He rose to his feet, but he was clearly injured.

Walbridge was in pain, but somehow descended again into the engine room. There was work to be done, machinery to be fixed. Everyone on board was needed. The captain could no longer delegate. Injured or not, he and his hands were needed, too.

Nothing about this trip was going as planned. The captain was hurt, pumps malfunctioned, increasing amounts of water entered the ship, and a hurricane of gigantic proportions bore down on *Bounty*. What more could possibly go wrong? The experienced crew members knew, which made them work all the harder to fix the pumps.

CHAPTER 7

Rising Water

Bounty, which earlier had been making ten knots—double her normal cruising speed—was now getting by on one engine, the starboard unit. The port engine had stopped running. The starboard generator was powering the bilge pumps. The seas seemed to be getting worse by the hour.

On the weather deck, Prokosh and Hewitt were at the helm when they looked up and saw the fore course—the same sail that the crew had furled earlier—ripping down the middle. Prokosh yelled an alert that brought the injured Walbridge to the deck. A call for all hands went out as the captain relieved Prokosh on the helm. The captain began assembling a team to deal with the flailing canvas partway up the foremast.

It was near two o'clock in the afternoon and the wind was now blowing at fifty knots, howling through the rigging. In the engine room, all other sounds were overwhelmed by the hammering of the diesel engines. But Scornavacchi, working down in the bilge area, heard, from above, the latest call for all hands. He began hollering: "All hands! All hands!" as he had learned to do during his six months aboard.

When Scornavacchi arrived on the weather deck, Walbridge was selecting crew to go aloft as he and Hewitt wrestled with the helm. He wanted only the most experienced men aloft, he said. He chose Scornavacchi and three others.

The wind at their backs, they climbed to the top of the torn sail. The wind was plastering them against the rigging. But if they turned and tried to look into the wind, they would be blinded by driving rain.

Once they reached the fore course, the sailors couldn't hold on to the straining sail cloth as it was yanked from their grip. The men had taken extra lines with them to tie the sail tight against the yard. But they lacked the strength to secure it. Eventually they gave up and the wind ripped the heavy fabric like it was cheap toilet paper.

Now, the spanker, a fore-and-aft sail mounted on the aft side of the mizzen mast and used to stabilize the ship's track, was flailing out of control. The ripped sail took with it splintered, swordlike sections of the spars that swung like medieval weapons in the gale.

Four climbers raced down to the deck, where the whole crew was now gathered in an attempt to control the treacherous spanker gaff. Scornavacchi grabbed a line but was lifted up off the deck. Four other crew members grabbed the line, and finally, with Scornavacchi hooking his toes under the lip of the roof over the great cabin, they managed to pull the shattered rigging to the deck, where they tied it down.

When the excitement subsided, Scornavacchi climbed down the forward stairs from the tween deck to the forecastle (the forward part of the ship) to resume his work. He found water three inches above the sole boards in the locker, and when the boat rolled, he felt his body rise in the air, seeming to float, and smash into a bulkhead. He collected tools and climbed back to the tween deck.

Other crew members tried to resume their naps. At about four o'clock, a large wave slammed into *Bounty*'s rear corner near where Laura Groves was sleeping. It was loud, like a dump truck hitting a house. Water came in the great cabin windows.

Around this time, Jessica Black began serving more macaroni and cheese for the dinner meal. Contained in bowls, the food was difficult to eat because the crew struggled to remain upright. Their efforts were aided when Walbridge went to watch Third Mate Cleveland and directed him to heave to. The practice of heaving to means that the ship will be virtually standing still, simply drifting with the wind and waves.

When the maneuver was completed, *Bounty* settled on a somewhat more even keel but rocking in the big waves.

Still, there was more work to be done. The starboard generator was surging and the electrical current throughout the boat was uneven. Walbridge ordered all nonessential electrical circuits turned off.

Fuel filters on all of the engines needed to be changed, and now the crew discovered that the supply of filters they'd received back in New London were wrong for the job.

Svendsen and Walbridge went down to the engine room, where the pumps were losing the battle with the rising water. The first mate suggested to the captain that it was time to let the coast guard know about *Bounty's* condition. Walbridge told him he felt it was more impor-tant to focus their efforts on getting the machinery running.

But Svendsen was extremely alarmed by the danger-ous strength of the storm and the problems aboard the *Bounty*. When Walbridge took no action, Svendsen went on deck with the ship's satellite telephone and attempted to call home base on Long Island.

Shouting into the wind, he called out *Bounty*'s loca-tion, not knowing if he had been heard.

The call had gone through. The home base called a coast guard number and relayed the message.

No one ashore knew the exact nature of the ship's dis-tress. In fact, few aboard *Bounty* knew everything that was happening on the ship's various decks. Once night arrived, the string of small events that had been accumulating all day had grown into a tangled ball.

The coast guard had told the office manager to tell the crew to activate their Emergency Position Indicating Radio Beacon (EPIRB). Soon an electronic signal was radi-ating from the ship, triggering a passing satellite, which relayed the ship's position to antennae ashore. Now the coast guard had a live indication where *Bounty* was—and that she was still floating.

At nine o'clock Sunday evening, Robin Walbridge

finally sent an email to the coast guard that acknowledged there were problems aboard *Bounty*.

"We are taking on water," he typed. "Will probably need assistance in the morning. Satellite phone is not working very good. We have activated the EPIRB. We are not in danger tonight, but if conditions don't improve on the boat, we will be in danger tomorrow. We can only run the generator for a short time. I just found out the fuel oil filters you got were the wrong filters. Let me know when you have contacted the USCG [US Coast Guard] so we can shut the EPIRB off. The boat is doing great but we can't dewater."

Just a few minutes later *Bounty*'s electronics started to fail. The ship still had sporadic power, but communication by email, satellite phone, and long-range radio was no longer possible. The situation was going from bad to worse.

PART II

CHAPTER 8

Wes McIntosh and the C-130

Commander Billy Mitchell, the Response Department Head for Coast Guard Sector North Carolina, faced his first big decision. He needed more information about the *Bounty*'s situation, taking on water with no power, out in the hurricane. The quickest way to do that would be to send out an aircraft. *That* would be dangerous, but to wait for improvements in the weather might be even more dangerous—and spell the end for the *Bounty*.

Mitchell and his team had determined there were no ships or coast guard cutters in the area that could help the *Bounty*. After much discussion, the decision was made to launch a C-130 aircraft and leave it to the discretion of the pilot to judge the winds to see how close he or she could fly to the foundering ship.

———◆———

C-130 Commander Frank "Wes" McIntosh was sprawled on the bed in his hotel room watching Sunday night football. His aircraft had been pre-positioned at Raleigh-Durham International Airport where potential crosswinds would be less troublesome than at Coast Guard Station Elizabeth City. The thirty-three-year-old pilot thought it might be a quiet night. With the hurricane dominating the news for the last three days he surmised all vessels would either be in port or far away from the swirling storm.

When his phone rang at 9:15 p.m., McIntosh realized he was dead wrong. On the line was the Elizabeth City Operations Duty Officer Todd Farrell.

"Hey, Wes," said Farrell, "we got a case for you . . . So start mobilizing."

"Okay, we'll get ready."

———◆———

Wes McIntosh seemed destined to be a pilot. Growing up in Beaufort, South Carolina, he watched F-18 military jets fly to and from the nearby Marine Corps Air Station, wondering what it would be like to be in one of those planes. His family also attended Blue Angels air shows, and he pictured himself in the cockpit, guiding the streaking aircraft across a cloudless sky. So it was no surprise when, a few years later, after graduating from Georgia Tech on an ROTC scholarship program, he accepted a commission in the navy and immediately started flight school.

Once he graduated, he started flying E-6Bs—modified Boeing 707s whose primary mission was to function as a communications platform in case of a ballistic missile attack on the United States. After three years of flying E-6Bs, McIntosh went on to be a flight instructor in military-training aircraft, logging 1,500 hours of training sorties in a three-and-a-half-year period. At the end of that tour, he had a choice to make: stay with the navy in a series of non-flying roles of increasing management responsibility, or transition to the coast guard where he could continue flying. The decision was easy—he wanted to stay in the sky, and in 2010, McIntosh joined the coast guard as a pilot of C-130s.

Now, with orders to mobilize his crew for a night flight to *Bounty*, McIntosh was glad he had already flown on several coast guard search and rescue missions. None of them, however, involved flying into a hurricane.

It was up to McIntosh to determine just how far into the storm he could fly before the hurricane winds overwhelmed both aircraft and crew.

Fortunately, the Lockheed C-130J "Super Hercules" was one tough aircraft. The coast guard found the aircraft to be extremely durable and reliable, and the C-130 had already become the primary fixed-winged aircraft used for search and rescue.

On the flight to *Bounty*, Wes McIntosh was the aircraft commander, and Mike Myers his copilot. They were supported by five other crew members: flight mechanic Hector Rios, mission system operators (MSOs) Joshua Adams and Joshua Vargo, drop-master Jesse Embert, and basic air crewman Eric Laster.

The flight mechanic sat directly behind the pilots, and the MSOs, who work with a variety of electronics, such as navigation and radio systems, were stationed just aft of the cockpit. The drop-master and basic air crewman occupied the spacious cargo compartment, and during the search, they would scan the ocean from their perch at two side windows. If Embert or Laster were fortunate enough to make visual contact with *Bounty*, it was their responsibility to deploy any needed equipment, such as rafts, dewatering pumps, survival suits, radios, or flares, which were all housed in floating, watertight containers.

The two men would do so by opening the ramp door at the rear of the aircraft, where they could push the equipment out the door. In light winds, they would attach parachutes, but Embert and Laster knew that in the hurricane the gear had to go without parachutes to avoid having it sail hundreds of yards from the intended target. Should they need to deploy a data-marker buoy, which measures drift rates and gives location fixes, this could be done through smaller side doors. Dropping any equipment, however, would not be easy, because to do so would require both men to be on their feet as the plane passed through turbulence.

By 10:00 p.m. the crew was onboard the idling aircraft, anxiously wondering just how bad the winds would become once they entered the enormous reach of Sandy. Already, a warning light blinked, alerting them that the anti-icing element on the propellers had failed.

The pilots conferred, and McIntosh announced over the internal communications system that they would fly out toward the *Bounty* at seven thousand feet but no higher, because icing might occur.

As they barreled down the runway and the aircraft

climbed into the black sky, a bit of rain splattered on the windscreen. McIntosh and Myers, both wearing night-vision goggles, guided the plane to the southeast.

The flight was unusually quiet after takeoff, until an air traffic controller from Raleigh-Durham broke the silence asking, "Hey, are you guys heading into Sandy?"

McIntosh responded in the affirmative, and the controller said, "Well, good luck to you."

Then another system malfunctioned, this one concerning the weather radar. McIntosh informed the MSOs sitting behind him, that he would be relying on them to use a different system—which McIntosh and Myers could not see—to assist them during the flight.

They continued cruising, now over the open ocean, and McIntosh thought, *Well, at least the malfunctions aren't serious enough for us to abort, but there better not be any-more. Not tonight.*

CHAPTER 9

Problems Everywhere

The entire crew on the *Bounty* was diligently working to solve the mounting problems on the ship. There was now no orderly watch system, no organized work party, no real sense of command. But there was determined motivation to save *Bounty*, save themselves.

The second mate, Matt Sanders, was in the heat and noise of the engine room. He had gone there to keep the bilge pumps running, but instead of bringing the flooding under control, he was wrestling with various mechanical problems, even as the water level rose.

When the starboard generator began surging and its power output fell, it was decided that the fuel filters needed to be changed even though the new filters were not a perfect fit. Sanders, a tall, athletically built man, took on the job.

The filter on the starboard generator's diesel engine was on the back side. To get to it, Sanders had to wedge himself behind the hot engine and get in a position where he could twist the filter free.

First, the generator had to be shut down. This meant the ship had no electrical current, and except for flashlights, *Bounty* went dark.

Sanders got into position and removed the old filter. Then First Mate Svendsen handed him a replacement filter. It took a while for Sanders to get the new filter seated properly.

With the new filter in place, Sanders was able to get the generator running. It started right up. Finally, something mechanical responded the way it was supposed to.

But the water level had risen dramatically, inch by inch, until it was thigh- to waist-deep on the starboard side. Sanders went to the tween deck where he found Walbridge. There was dangerous electrical current in the water. Sanders asked permission to shut down the generator.

Permission granted, Sanders returned to the engine room and cut the fuel supply, stopping the engine and its generator.

Once again, the ship was dark. There was only one hope—to get the port generator back in action. Sanders now changed the fuel filter on the port generator, bled the air out of the fuel system, cleaned the fuel injectors, and tried to restart the engine.

Nothing.

After consulting with Walbridge, Sanders went to the engine control panel. He disabled an electrical switch, and this time, when he tried to start the engine, it fired up. The lights went on inside *Bounty* for the first time in more than an hour.

Sanders had been in the engine room for more than six hours now. He was alarmed that blue arcs of electricity were visible as the water continued to rise. Moreover, the engine room sole boards were floating and slamming from side to side as *Bounty* rolled. The water was waist- to chest-deep on Sanders, who felt the atmosphere was dangerous. He left the engine room and got a glass of water.

Looking for a place to be useful, Josh Scornavacchi descended to the engine room but found it now flooded and abandoned. He went to his cabin in the aft crew quarters to fetch some tools. On the way, he saw that

Walbridge, Sanders, and Barksdale were crouched over a small gasoline pump. The crew called it a trash pump and it had never been used but was stored, wrapped in plastic, for an emergency. They had placed a hose from the pump running aft thirty feet to a great cabin window. Another hose went from the tween deck down into the engine room.

But the trash pump wasn't working yet, despite the efforts of the three officers.

◄█►

Earlier, Adam Prokosh was feeling pretty confident. But then the power went out and the lights went off, and he was saying to himself, *What the heck is going on?*

He went to the engine room, where he found Walbridge, Sanders, and Barksdale—what he considered the entirety of the ship's engineering skills. It crossed Prokosh's mind that the high bilge water was filled with small pieces of debris. If the guys in the engine room were successful, then there would be a need to clean the strainers in the pump system. He went to the galley and asked Jessica Black to borrow a colander. Back in the bilge, he began scooping.

Then Scornavacchi joined him in the bilge and asked how he could help.

"You can take over this job. Take this colander and I'll grab another," Prokosh replied. He climbed back to the tween deck and asked the cook if he could borrow another colander.

"Use whatever you need," Black said.

Now Prokosh followed Black out of the galley, heading aft in the vast, open saloon, toward the engine room ladder. The cook, only four days into her tall-ship career, was holding on to the long jack line that earlier had been strung the length of the cabin. Prokosh, one step behind and talking with Black, had the colander in one hand but wasn't holding the jack line with his free hand. A huge wave slammed into the side of *Bounty*, and the ship rocked violently to starboard.

Prokosh was airborne. An unguided missile, his body flew toward the low, starboard side. His head and back smashed into a chest bolted to the floor. He collapsed in a heap where he landed.

Black thought Prokosh had a concussion, and she raced to find the first mate.

Other crew members found a mattress and Prokosh

was rolled onto it. The damage was extensive. Prokosh had suffered a compression fracture in a vertebra, three broken ribs, a separated shoulder, and head trauma. He would be of no further use in the effort to save *Bounty*.

Jessica Black had no duties other than to keep the crew fed. From time to time, she got reports from crew members about the breakdowns, the flooding, and the injuries. Much of her information came from Claudene Christian, who visited the galley frequently. Scornavacchi called Christian the crew's "spy" because she listened in on conversations among the officers and delivered their private thoughts to her crewmates.

On that Sunday evening, though, Black was focused on preparing dinner rather than gossip. Once again, due to the instability of the boat, the food had to be something that could be served in a bowl. Mac and cheese was her choice for a second time. But she wanted there to be a vegetable, and she chose frozen peas. They could be heated in the microwave.

Then she turned on the microwave.

Sparks shot out. There was smoke. Black had her own small disaster right there in the galley. There was an arc, like lightning, but no fire. Doug Faunt was summoned, and he solved the problem and dinner preparations continued.

Normally, there were three shifts for meals, one from each watch. But on Sunday night, there were few diners. Someone told Black there were so many problems that people didn't have time to eat on schedule. So Black made up bundles of bottled water and snacks and began delivering them to crew members immersed in their work.

As she circulated, Black saw Chris Barksdale, the engineer. He was seasick but still working. She found him struggling with the trash pump at the top of the engine room ladder. Black stopped to help him, holding the trash pump for well over an hour while Barksdale tried to get it started.

The small pump refused to work. It was as if the *Bounty* itself was having its own mutiny against the efforts of the crew.

CHAPTER 10

Unseen Punches

After half an hour of flying in turbulence, the crew of the C-130 was alarmed by the violent gusts of wind that battered the aircraft. Buffeting winds caused the plane to suddenly drop ten to twenty feet, leaving everyone feeling like their stomachs were somewhere north of their eyeballs. No one talked, and several crew members tried to fight off nausea.

After another twenty minutes of flying, McIntosh tried to raise *Bounty* on the radio.

"*Bounty*, this is Coast Guard C-130 on channel sixteen. How copy? Over."

"C-130 this is *Bounty*, we read you loud and clear."

Startled by the immediate response and the clarity, McIntosh, thankful that the ship was afloat and its battery-operated radio was working, gave a thumbs-up to Myers.

"This is C-130. Request to know position, number of people on board, and nature of your distress."

McIntosh assumed he was talking to the captain, but it was First Mate John Svendsen on the radio. In a calm and professional voice, Svendsen gave the commander their position. He explained that sixteen people were on board, that the generators were down, and the ship was drifting. He then added, "We have six feet of water on board and are taking on an additional one foot of water per hour."

McIntosh and copilot Mike Myers exchanged glances. This news was worse than they had expected.

"What is your plan of action?" asked McIntosh to *Bounty*.

"We think we can make it to dawn. If we don't have assistance at 7:30 a.m. we will abandon ship in the daylight."

The C-130 was still approximately fifty miles away from *Bounty*. Although the wind strengthened with each passing mile, the commander felt it was well within the capabilities of his aircraft. McIntosh had flown in worse. But in the meantime, he worried that *Bounty*'s battery-operated radio might die. He needed to be close enough to actually see the ship to make sure it was still afloat.

Through his night-vision goggles, McIntosh could see the tops of clouds, and they didn't appear to be the cumulonimbus type known as thunderstorm clouds. The winds rose to eighty knots and the turbulence worsened. But McIntosh didn't think the weather was convective, the type that could sheer the plane's wings off in a blink of an eye.

McIntosh guided the aircraft even deeper into the storm toward the foundering ship, asking his MSOs if they could see *Bounty* on radar. They answered in the negative; the waves were simply too big. McIntosh then asked Myers to take over the controls and to slowly descend toward the location of the ship. That would free up McIntosh to radio Sector North Carolina, and give them a complete briefing.

As Myers decreased altitude, the wind eased to sixty knots, yet the gusts became more frequent and severe, causing the plane to shudder and lurch. The autopilot had long since been switched off and Myers flew by hand controls. Descending through walls of clouds, the aircraft pitched violently to the left as the wind shifted direction. The clouds released their load of rain, pelting the windshield so hard, the pilots felt like it could shatter at any moment. Despite wearing noise-cancelling headsets, the pilots clearly heard the roar of the pounding, and now knew they really were in the grip of the monster hurricane.

With the rain, the turbulence increased to yet another level, and the C-130's wings flexed up and down by as much as four feet, as unseen punches rocked the plane. Anything not strapped down hurled across the cockpit and the cargo area.

Suddenly, a gust of wind, stronger than anything yet experienced, hit the plane on the nose, shooting it upward two hundred feet. Then, as soon as the gust passed, the aircraft plummeted four hundred feet before Myers could bring it back under control. Anyone feeling nauseated earlier was now vomiting. Torrents of rain made for zero visibility.

The crew in the back could only sit tight and put their faith, and their lives, in the two men in the cockpit.

The *Bounty* crew was ecstatic to learn that a coast guard plane had made radio contact with John Svendsen and was just a few miles away. It gave them hope at a time when conditions were deteriorating fast. Maybe the plane could drop pumps, maybe they could find a commercial ship to assist in a rescue, but most important, they were no longer alone in the storm.

In the meantime, there was still a battle to be fought onboard the ship.

And although there was no official proclamation, the bilge and the lower deck were surrendered to the rising water well before midnight.

McIntosh took the controls back from Myers and put the plane in a racetrack pattern, coaxing the C-130 slowly downward toward a five-hundred-foot altitude. Going lower than that was not an option, not with the aircraft rising and falling precipitously with each sudden wind gust. He had been told *Bounty*'s masts were approximately one-hundred-fifty feet tall, and he didn't want to verify that information by crashing into them.

Suddenly, through a break in the clouds the commander saw waves—large waves—some cresting at an astonishing thirty feet. But what really got his attention was that the waves were coming from all directions, as if the giant rollers were battling one another for supremacy.

The night-vision goggles made the scene especially

eerie. The waves and sky were a dark green, but the streaking foam and churning wave tops were bright and clearly visible, clashing and smashing into one another. McIntosh wondered how in the world any vessel, much less one taking on considerable water, could stay afloat in such chaos.

Up ahead and off to the right a beam of light rose from the ocean, and McIntosh carefully banked the plane in that direction. It was a handheld flashlight a sailor on the *Bounty* was shining at the aircraft. Myers, sitting in the right seat, saw the ship first, and with awe in his voice, said, "There she is."

The ship was out of McIntosh's line of sight, and he asked the copilot what it looked like.

"Well," said Myers, "it looks like a big pirate ship in the middle of a hurricane."

As the C-130 roared past *Bounty*, McIntosh made a wide arching turn to bring the aircraft back over the ship. This time McIntosh had a perfect view of the vessel, and he thought how Myers's description was perfect.

The ship was listing about 45 degrees to starboard and enormous waves smashed into her, sending spray up into the sky, where it was snatched by the wind. *This is surreal,* he thought, *the ship looks like it's part of a movie set.*

His glimpse lasted only a couple seconds before

the aircraft zipped past *Bounty*, but McIntosh had seen enough. He could tell that the ship was in far worse trouble than merely taking on water. It seemed to the commander that the very next wave might put the vessel completely on its side. McIntosh immediately radioed this information back to his command post.

CHAPTER 11

The Dangerous Hours

Midnight came, and *Bounty*'s entire crew was gathered on the tween deck. The water was six feet or more above where the engine room sole boards, now floating, once made a floor. Giant, lethal waves sloshed within the fore and aft crew quarters and all the other compartments at that lowest level. Everywhere below, sole boards slammed into bulkheads, unrestrained.

On the weather deck, conditions were worse. *Bounty* heeled steeply to starboard, her deck slick, her bow bucking up and plunging down. There was no need to be on deck. There were no sails to man, no forward progress to threaten a collision.

Everything that could be salvaged from the compartments below the tween deck had already been brought up and was piled in heaps.

Everyone on board *Bounty* at this point was exhausted. Sleeping had been difficult to impossible for more than twenty-four hours, and the situation wasn't going to improve. Walbridge gave instructions for everyone who had no duties to get some rest.

Almost everyone aboard knew *Bounty* was doomed. The question was how long could it stay afloat.

The coast guard had informed *Bounty* that there were no ships closer than eight hours away. The old ship was on its own, and the water kept rising.

Robin Walbridge let the crew know that when—not if—the water level rose to the tween deck, everyone would be required to get into an immersion suit. The immersion suit would help keep their bodies warm in the event the vessel sank and the crew had to abandon ship.

It was a tribute to Walbridge's foresight that *Bounty* had at least thirty of what are popularly called survival suits. They were made out of neoprene, red in color, and nicknamed "Gumby suits" for the way they looked like the clay cartoon character. The survival suits provide floatation and warmth and visibility.

Some crew members had already picked out a suit and put it on immediately, while most waited for the captain's orders.

While the water was still below the tween deck floor, First Mate Svendsen told Bosun Groves to distribute seasick pills to the crew. She began making the rounds, offering a pill to each crew member. Walbridge, who was having trouble walking but was still mobile, declined. Barksdale, already seasick, took one and vomited.

Groves organized a crew to locate additional safety gear. They brought all of the life jackets from a cabin and tied them together so that, if thrown into the water, the orange fabric of the jacket would make a large, visible target for possible rescuers. They filled plastic construction bags with bottles of water, canned food, and personal dry bags and tied them closed so they would float.

The power proceeded to fail and then return, so the work was conducted under the light of individual head lamps. Almost no one was napping. There was too much work to be done.

The crew was vividly aware of their precarious situation.

Scornavacchi was nervous, uncertain. On the one hand, there was clarity in the situation. The water was close to the level of the tween deck, and the time was almost at hand when he and the crew would put on the immersion suits. But when would the evacuation happen? Only time would tell.

Most of all, though, Scornavacchi was tired. Thinking was difficult. The morning before, the captain had promised a day without work. But then, disastrous events demanded more work. Manning the pumps constantly. Climbing the rigging.

That was Sunday, all day. Now on Monday morning, the work was still ongoing. Scornavacchi still did not nap.

Meanwhile, some water accumulated on the low side of the tween deck, where an injured Prokosh lay on a mattress. Claudene Christian, who had been visiting him regularly, helped him to his feet. She supported him as he climbed the sloped deck to a cabin on the port side. There he was put on a bunk somewhat dryer than the soggy mattress.

It was now about three o'clock in the morning, and Walbridge called his crew together near the Nav Shack. He stood on the stairway and looked down—as he had done four afternoons before in New London. The captain asked them to brainstorm to answer a question: At what point did we lose control?

No one offered Walbridge an answer. Indeed, most of

the crew were so mentally wasted that few even knew a question was being asked.

The meeting broke up, and many in the crew, unwilling to embrace sleep, gravitated to the only place where there was still some action: the trash pump. Now the pump was on the weather deck. Barksdale and others worked feverishly, yanking the pull cord, attempting to start it. Suddenly, the pump sputtered to life.

The crew cheered wildly.

Thirty seconds later, the pump—and then the crew—fell quiet.

Now the muted conversations inside *Bounty* centered on one theme. The crew would wait until daylight, then conduct an orderly transfer into the two twenty-five-person life rafts mounted at the stern.

Scornavacchi, waiting in the area where he had helped pile the immersion suits, looked into the last cabin on the port side—Walbridge's state room. He saw the captain holding a picture, staring at it. It seemed to be a portrait of Claudia McCann, his wife.

Scornavacchi did not intrude on the captain's thoughts. He moved on.

Moments later, Prokosh got the word that Walbridge had issued the order: Put on your immersion suits. He crawled across the slant of the deck to a suit. Lying in pain from his injured back, he shook the suit from its bag, unrolled it, and began pulling it over his shoes.

His pain was too intense for him to stand, so Prokosh rested. He watched other crew members mill about in their ridiculously bulky suits.

The officers pulled on the legs of the suits and zipped the fronts up to their waists, leaving their hands free to help the rest of the crew.

Even now, calm prevailed. There was no urgency to get on deck. *Bounty* was riding on a severe tilt with the water now at least ankle deep on the high side of the tween deck.

Word spread among crew members that climbing harnesses and life jackets were to be worn outside the immersion suits. The coast guard, circling above now in the C-130, routinely asks a vessel in distress whether its occupants are wearing life jackets. There was no direct order from Walbridge to don a life jacket, but most crew members heard the spreading word. At the same time, the explanation circulated that harnesses would allow them to clip together once they had abandoned ship. They could bring along personal "ditch" bags, shackled to the harness, so they could save possessions they felt were vital.

The actual process of getting into harnesses and life

jackets once the crew members were inside the immersion suits was cumbersome. One crew member had a multi-tool that had a set of pliers. He used this to help tighten harnesses that the wearers were unable to adjust on their own.

Doug Faunt, in his cabin forward of Walbridge's, put on an extra layer of warm clothing before he got into his suit.

Claudene Christian, in the next cabin, stepped into a size small.

Jessica Hewitt reminded people around her to strap the legs tight with the Velcro straps around the ankles so that walking would be easier.

Joshua Scornavacchi felt lost in his size-medium suit.

The suits would keep them warm if they were in the ocean, but the crew knew that if they couldn't get into life rafts, the enormous waves would drive them under and drown them. Their best hope was that *Bounty* stayed afloat until morning's first light, and then they could do an orderly evacuation into the life rafts. But was that hope realistic?

CHAPTER 12

"We Are in Survival Suits"

McIntosh and Myers continued guiding the C-130 through the turbulence, hoping that each time they tried to reach *Bounty* the ship would still be afloat.

"*Bounty*, this is the Coast Guard C-130, do you copy?"

"This is *Bounty*, we hear you loud and clear."

"We can finally see you, and we are going to relay your predicament back to headquarters. In the meantime, we're going to see about getting pumps to you and locating ships that can head to your position."

McIntosh played through the procedure of dropping pumps to a vessel taking on water. The pumps could be used to vacuum out water from the ship. Normally, dropping a pump from the aircraft is done from an altitude of two hundred feet, a height from which the pump has a realistic chance of making it to the vessel. The pump is in a watertight canister, which has a long trailing line attached to it. If all goes as planned, the pump lands in the water and the line lands on the vessel's deck. There, a sailor can grab it and haul the pump to the ship.

McIntosh thought about the sixty-five-knot winds and the enormous waves. He concluded that in those conditions, a pump would have a small chance of being recovered by the crew. It might even add a whole new element of danger for everyone involved.

If McIntosh took the plane down to two hundred feet, he risked getting his entire crew killed, so he immediately dismissed that notion. He might get lucky by successfully releasing the pump from five hundred feet. But having a *Bounty* crew member scramble out on the steeply angled deck to retrieve the line might cause them to be swept overboard.

"I worried the pump would make things worse," recalled McIntosh. "The seventy-pound pump might plummet directly onto the deck like a missile, crashing through the planking and opening yet another spot for water to enter the vessel." Adding to his concern was that the heavy rain made visibility of the ship impossible until they were directly over it.

McIntosh made another pass over the ship. When it briefly came into view, he noticed that the starboard side rail was now completely submerged. He made up his mind not to drop the pump. Because the *Bounty* was taking on a foot of water an hour, McIntosh knew it needed a much larger pump than he had on the plane. Dropping a small one would barely have an impact, and it wasn't worth the potential danger to a *Bounty* crew member. He relayed his decision back to Sector North Carolina, and they agreed.

"*Bounty*, this is CG C-130, how copy?"

"Loud and clear."

"In these winds, it would be next to impossible to get a pump to you. Even if we got the trailing line on your deck, retrieving this one small pump would put the lives of your crew members in jeopardy."

"Roger, we understand."

"What are your plans?"

"We are in survival suits. We have multiple EPIRBs, and have two large life rafts. We hope to make it until daylight when we can more safely get in the rafts. Each raft will have an EPIRB and a handheld VHS radio, but we can't guarantee they will work if they get wet. Are there any ships on the way?"

McIntosh had to tell them the truth. "Negative."

There was an awkward silence, and then Myers spoke with Svendsen, reviewing the plans for abandoning ship safely.

When the conversation was over with Sector, McIntosh used his internal communication system to see how the rest of his crew were doing.

One crew member responded, "Sir, I know a few of us are feeling pretty sick."

"Roger," said McIntosh. "We're going to climb back up in altitude where the gusts aren't as powerful. We'll still have excellent communications with the sailing vessel."

McIntosh notified Sector that the crew and aircraft were taking a beating, but that they could continue the mission. Sector then confirmed that because the *Bounty*'s command thought they could make it to morning, it would be best to have the helicopter launch just before dawn. It was simply too dangerous to send a helo into Sandy at night.

"Roger," said McIntosh. "But remember we are going to need at least two helicopters with sixteen people in life rafts."

Myers eased the aircraft back up to seven thousand feet and continued the racetrack pattern over *Bounty*. Every now and then either Myers or McIntosh would ask the *Bounty* for an update.

Conditions were more stable at the higher altitude and McIntosh hoped his crew, who were being knocked around in the belly of the plane, would get a better handle on their motion sickness. He knew they weren't going home anytime soon.

After fifteen or twenty minutes, the commander decided it was time to descend to five hundred feet for a visual on *Bounty*. McIntosh hoped to see the ship listing at the same angle as before, but instead the vessel was farther on its side, with more green water sweeping over the deck.

McIntosh became increasingly anxious about *Bounty's* chances of making it to morning. Adding to his concern, Svendsen asked if any helicopters had launched. McIntosh responded that the helicopters would arrive in the morning, if possible, because the hurricane winds were extremely dangerous for a helo to fly into at night to try a rescue.

It was now about 4:00 a.m., and the commander had the feeling that conditions were deteriorating on the *Bounty* faster than the sailors had anticipated. He decided it would be prudent to call Air Station Elizabeth City and tell Todd Farrell at the Operations Center exactly what was going on. McIntosh needed to describe the conditions in detail so the helicopter pilots would have as much information as possible.

To McIntosh's surprise a helicopter copilot named Jane Pena picked up the phone rather than Farrell. McIntosh explained what was happening. "Things are getting worse onboard the vessel. Before too long, there will probably be people in the water."

He had Pena's full attention—she was part of the "ready" crew that would launch if need be. McIntosh went on to describe the powerful wind gusts and the three-story waves crashing in confused seas. As they ended the conversation, McIntosh added, "We are going to need another C-130 out here. We're running low on fuel. They should launch as soon as possible in case the worst happens."

Pena hung up the phone. She looked at both Todd Farrell and Lieutenant Commander Steve Cerveny, who were standing next to her, listening to her side of the conversation. "McIntosh thinks the sailors might have to abandon ship before dawn. And he needs another C-130 out there ASAP."

While Farrell got busy coordinating the next plane to launch, Cerveny said to Pena, "Well, I hope the *Bounty* can make it to morning, but let's get our aircraft and crew ready to go at a moment's notice, just in case."

Pena gave a tense nod. This would be her first major helicopter rescue, and the flying conditions would be unlike anything she'd ever experienced. She could feel the excitement and anticipation building in her, and hoped they would launch soon.

Onboard the C-130, Myers was now talking with Sector. He was asked to relay a message to *Bounty*. Myers picked up the radio.

"Another C-130 is coming. Would two P-100 pumps be enough to dewater the ship and keep it afloat?"

Svendsen responded with a sense of humor. "Two P-100s would be nice, but two P-250s would even be better."

Myers sensed that behind the gallows humor, Svendsen was deadly serious that only the largest of pumps could even have a chance at saving *Bounty*. His heart went out to the mariners. Myers stayed on the radio, talking and trying to keep the sailor's spirits up.

"It was painful," Myers later recounted, "to experience their highs and lows."

CHAPTER 13

A Rushed and Urgent Call

The rising water had reached the tween deck: It was time to leave that sheltered space. If the boat capsized and the crew was in the tween deck they would be trapped there. One by one, the crew members filed up to the weather deck. Some went forward to brace themselves on structures in front of the Nav Shack. Others headed aft, toward the life rafts.

The wind had abated some, to perhaps forty knots—still strong enough to make the rigging sing and roar and to stifle conversation with its volume. But the seas were still huge. With her lowest deck filled with a heavy ballast of salt water, *Bounty* rode relatively smoothly. And now, there was a full moon above, lighting the edges of the racing clouds. It was enough light that the crew could see their ship leaning 45 degrees to starboard. They could also see the waves all around them, like they were sitting deep in a valley with dark mountains on every side and only the silvery sky above.

As they made their way to the weather deck, some of the crew members formed a line. They handed up the gear that the bosun had assembled in plastic bags, as well as the life jackets that were tied together in orange rafts.

Walbridge and Svendsen remained in the Nav Shack as the exodus continued. Then the captain asked crewmember Anna Sprague, one of the last to go on deck, to help him into the top of his survival suit. Then he followed her to the weather deck, which slanted up like a steeply pitched roof, and sat down, waiting for morning to arrive, the time when he would dictate an orderly departure.

Moments later, Svensen came on deck. He had been watching the starboard rail. It had dipped under the waves. There was so much water in the ship that *Bounty* was leaning farther and farther on its side. The first mate knew his captain wanted to avoid abandoning ship during the night, and instead wait for daylight when it would be safer to board the life rafts. But now the rail was fully submerged, and Svendsen sensed that the time was at hand.

"*It's time to go,*" Svendsen told Walbridge.

The captain did not respond, so the first mate waited a half minute and repeated his suggestion, his plea.

Again Walbridge ignored the warning.

After Svendsen repeated the request a third time, Walbridge finally agreed. Svendsen returned to the Nav Shack to alert the C-130 flying above. The word began to spread across the ship. The crew would launch the two rafts and attempt a controlled descent from the deck.

But it was too late.

Suddenly, the ship leaned hard to starboard, dropping its masts in the ocean, bringing its deck to vertical.

McIntosh and Myers alternated flying the C-130 above the ship. Sometimes they flew at five hundred feet to get a visual and sometimes at seven thousand to give their team less of a pounding from the storm.

Suddenly at 4:45 a.m., Svendsen's voice boomed into the cockpit of the C-130. "We are abandoning ship! We are abandoning ship!"

McIntosh's heart skipped a beat. All previous calls had

been calm and collected, but this one was rushed and urgent. He grabbed the radio, "*Bounty*, this is CG 130. Tell us what is happening."

Silence.

Chills went down McIntosh's back. "*Bounty*, this is CG 130. How copy?"

Silence.

"*Bounty*, are you getting into life rafts?"

Dead air.

McIntosh switched to another channel. "*Bounty*, this is Coast Guard C-130. How copy?"

No response.

McIntosh cursed under his breath and made eye contact with Myers. He knew this was not the orderly abandoning of ship everyone had hoped for. It was clear Svendsen had had just a second to get his distress call out. Something sudden and cataclysmic must have happened, and McIntosh wondered if anyone got off the ship alive.

Adrenaline shot through every vein of Wes McIntosh, and he had to fight back a surge of nervous energy. He had formed a bond with the people on *Bounty*, particularly with Svendsen on the radio. McIntosh thought, *This whole night it's been just us and the* Bounty *alone out in this black mess, and now it might be all over. It sure didn't sound like they had time to get in life rafts.* McIntosh was certain the ship had capsized, but the people could be either in the water or trapped inside the ship.

◤◼◼◼◼◼◼◼◼◼◼◼◼◼

Onboard *Bounty,* anyone not thoroughly braced instantly fell into the sea. Others clung to the nearest fixed object, desperately postponing their own fall into the ocean.

Laura Groves had just helped Dan Cleveland into the top half of his immersion suit when *Bounty* lurched. Then she found herself in the ocean.

Joshua Scornavacchi had settled on the port side of the fife rail around the main mast, his feet standing on the rail, his back lying on the tilted deck. Claudene Christian was beside him, and she smiled at him. Then she scampered aft, toward another group of crew members.

Scornavacchi closed his eyes, and a moment later when he opened them, he saw his fellow sailors hanging like so much laundry from various lines and railings. He worked his way down the rail toward the water and then he jumped.

Prokosh, at the stern behind the helm, saw the big steering wheel go under the water and thought, *This is where I get off.* He allowed himself to slide down onto the helm and then jumped toward a clear patch of water, hoping to avoid getting entangled in the rigging.

Jessica Hewitt had fallen asleep near the helm. She awoke to see water directly before her.

Jessica Black heard someone yell, "She's going!" and sensed what was happening. She wanted to be in control of her destiny, so she let go and fell into the sea.

Svendsen, still in the Nav Shack calling the coast guard, was caught by a flood of sea, a waterfall coming into the companionway. He fought against it, making it to the deck. Before him he saw Robin Walbridge, a life jacket strapped over his immersion suit, walking aft—walking, not crawling, because while the deck was vertical, there were horizontal surfaces like the fife rail.

The first mate found the nearest mast, now horizontal, and climbed along it, away from the deck, away from his captain, away from *Bounty*.

The plane was up at the seven-thousand-foot level. Myers took the controls and started descending, while one of the MSOs radioed Sector that the *Bounty* sailors were abandoning ship and communication had been lost.

Then McIntosh spoke on the internal communications system to his crew.

"They're abandoning ship. You know what we need to do now."

What they needed to do was get life rafts in the water immediately. This is where drop-master Jesse Embert and basic air crewman Eric Laster earned their pay, no matter how motion sick they were. The two men had eight-person life rafts and survival bags stuffed with water packs, patches for plugging potential holes in the life rafts, space blankets, whistles, flares, and strobe lights.

Staggering, they dragged the equipment toward the rear of the plane, losing their footing temporarily by the opened ramp.

Meanwhile, McIntosh calculated a release point while the MSOs worked the radio, making continuous callouts to the foundering vessel, hoping against all odds for an answer.

Embert's voice came over the internal communication set. "Mr. McIntosh, we have completed our checklist and have the equipment in place."

"Roger," answered McIntosh. "We are descending to five hundred feet and are depressurizing the plane." This would ensure that the ramp could be opened safely.

The C-130 barreled out of the clouds at one hundred fifty knots and the *Bounty* appeared below them. The ship lay flat on her side. Everyone in the aircraft stared out rain-slashed windows, trying to pick out survivors. Debris littered the ocean. One of the crew members shouted, "I see a raft!" Then another one hollered, "There's a second raft at the two o'clock position!"

The crew also saw multiple strobe lights blinking in the water. But they saw no survivors.

As the plane zoomed past the debris field, McIntosh banked it to return to the site. The aircraft groaned and shuddered, battered by varying wind gusts. McIntosh gave the ocean a wide berth, trying to keep the plane as close to five hundred feet as possible.

Meyers radioed Sector. "We've visually confirmed that the ship has capsized; it's on its side. We have seen two rafts, and many strobe lights in the water, but unsure where the people are. We are deploying our life rafts."

McIntosh gave Embert the okay to open the ramp door and told him they were circling back to the *Bounty*, where he would give the command to drop two rafts. A thousand feet of line connected the two rafts, with the hope that a survivor could grab the line and pull themselves along to safety. Embert and Laster began the process of opening the ramp, and the roar of the wind was deafening. Each man wore a harness with a tether fixed to the aircraft wall. Should they slip and fall out the ramp, this would prevent them from free-falling into the sea. They double-checked each other's harness and tether, just to make sure.

Moving the rafts to the open cargo doorway, the two men fought back their motion sickness as best they could. The rear of the aircraft took the brunt of the turbulence, and the men found it impossible to stand without holding on to the walls of the plane. Nausea got the best of one of the men, and he vomited, causing the rain-soaked floor by the ramp to become even more slippery.

Over the headset, McIntosh alerted Embert and Laster that they were coming up on the *Bounty* and to get ready.

When McIntosh saw the *Bounty* almost directly below them, he waited about five seconds, then ordered, "Drop! Drop! Drop!"

Embert and Laster shoved the first raft out the plane, counted off two seconds and then pushed the second into the black void. The two-second interval between the rafts was to insure they did not become tangled. They wanted the rafts to land in different spots with the tether between them.

Usually the drop-master can see if his drop is accurate,

but with pelting wind and darkness, the rafts were swallowed by the night before they hit the water. The two men inched back away from the doorway, thankful there was no mishap when they were at the outer lip of the ramp.

McIntosh circled back around and through his night-vision goggles could see that the two coast guard rafts had landed just where they had wanted them to, near the debris field. But the wind wasn't going to allow them to stay there for long. Although the rafts had drogue chutes designed to drag underwater and slow their drifting, the rafts still blew end over end.

CHAPTER 14

The First Raft

Order had turned into chaos. Shouts filled the air as *Bounty* crew members fell or jumped into the sea.

If they were going to survive, each crew member now had only themselves and their will to live—and the two small life rafts that had plunged overboard with the rest of them—to give them any hope.

When *Bounty* rolled to starboard and the water rose, Sanders saw Walbridge hit the water, and watched the captain get washed back and forth in the waves. Sanders was unable to give aid because his feet were trapped in the yards.

Christian was holding on nearby and shouted to Sanders, "What do I do? What do I do?"

"Claudene, you just have to go for it! You have to make your way aft and get clear of the boat!" Sanders shouted as he watched her begin to follow his directive.

A second or two later, Sanders freed his feet, and he too headed aft. When Christian was out of sight, he climbed past the big wooden wheel, then leaped off *Bounty*'s stern.

Sprague was able to stand on the yards when the deck tilted up to vertical. Without thinking, she jumped in the water, landing in front of the fallen mizzen mast. There she found crew member Mark Warner and, moments later, fellow crew member John Jones, and they saw a life raft canister and talked about deploying the packed raft.

Without warning, the mizzen mast began to rise, surfacing directly under Jones, whose legs straddled the spar. The ship rolled to port and the mast hoisted him into the air.

Doug Faunt had been one of the first on deck in his immersion suit, working his way back to the helm. As the water rose around him, he swam away from the ship, but not clear of its rigging. Twice, he was shoved under. He feared being drawn under permanently if the swamped ship plunged to the depths. Looking in every direction, he finally saw an inflated life raft and swam to it. It was too difficult to climb so he hung on to the edge. The water yanked him about and he separated his shoulder.

Jessica Black had come on deck shortly after Faunt. As she passed through the Nav Shack, Svendsen had strapped her life vest on. She ended up with her feet braced against the mizzen fife rail, near Scornavacchi. Suddenly, she was in the water, grasping for things to hold on to. At one point, Black came upon Scornavacchi, who was near a life raft canister. She tried to rip the raft's tether to deploy it, but she lost her grip and drifted away from the raft and Scornavacchi. She was aware of where one of the masts was slashing into the water and wanted to escape it, so she swam. Then she thought, *I'm clear of the ship, but where's the life raft?*

Some of the waves were bigger than others as Black swam blindly. When she rose to the crest of one huge wave, she looked down and saw before her, as if at the bottom of a hill, a life raft. She still had her life vest, but the waist strap had detached and the vest was beside her. Sighting the raft ahead, the cook stiffened her body and surfed down the face of the wave toward the raft. She worried she could overshoot her target—and lose the chance for survival that the raft presented.

Her aim was accurate, and when she reached the raft, she found Faunt.

Before Joshua Scornavacchi abandoned ship, he saw someone already in the water, as another person jumped overboard. He jumped, too, and when he did, someone—a woman still on the boat, he didn't know who—reached out and tried to grab his hand.

Instantly, he saw that the sea was littered with pieces of wood, trash—a sloshing soup. He reached to grab some floating debris, but it was torn from his grip. And in that first instant in the water, he felt himself being sucked under the ship, felt his boots being yanked from his feet inside his suit. In fact, he was being pulled bodily beneath the surface. A snarl of *Bounty*'s lines had wrapped around his ditch bag and was pulling him down.

His survival gear was threatening to kill him.

In his work as a white-water-rafting guide, Scornavac-chi had learned to escape when he found himself getting sucked under by down currents. The technique involved swimming while executing a barrel roll. Holding his breath, he tried the maneuver now. It didn't work because he couldn't get the bag untangled from the ropes that held it and couldn't undo the shackle that fastened it to his harness.

Saltwater mixed with diesel in Scornavacchi's mouth. He ran out of breath, started coughing underwater and involuntarily drew that foul mixture into his windpipe, perhaps his lungs. He felt his muscles quit working and believed he was drowning.

Anger filled him. He had promised his mother and his eleven-year-old brother that he wouldn't drown, and now he realized he would never see them again. Thoughts raced through his mind. If he was drowning, then everyone else from *Bounty* was probably dead. He couldn't understand why they hadn't boarded the rafts sooner.

Then the voice came. Maybe, he thought, it was God. It said, *It's not your time yet.* At that moment, the ditch bag released itself from his harness, and he swam to the sur-face, where he saw the big mound of emergency supplies. He swam to it, clutched at it with his hands. Then he tried to climb atop the pile, away from the snares of the sinking ship.

From out of the dark, Jessica Black appeared. It seemed she was asking him what to do. He urged her to climb on the pile with him. But just then, the main mast—he knew its bottom section alone weighed over six tons—slammed down on the pile, launching Scornavacchi into the air. When he fell back in the water, Black was gone.

Alone, he tried to swim away but got another line wrapped around his leg. He removed it, then saw the mizzen mast in the water nearby. He grabbed the spar and tried to pull himself away from the ship along it, to escape the debris. Suddenly, the mast began to rise from the water as the ship rolled. In rising, it lifted him out of the water thirty feet.

"Jump!" a male voice yelled. He didn't want to jump, but he did, landing in a clear patch of water.

In the distance, he saw a life raft canister, so he swam as hard as he could and reached it. As he worked to undo the canister, another crew member, John Jones, appeared and tried to yank the raft's tether to deploy it.

Jones and Scornavacchi worked on the raft canister but couldn't get it open. So they pushed it toward a spot where they thought there might be other crew members.

High above, strange-looking clouds raced south and east. Down in the troughs between the waves, it was quiet. The silence was startling after the endless hours aboard *Bounty* amid the cacophony of the ship and the storm.

Scornavacchi asked Jones if he had seen anyone else. He hadn't. All that was certain was that the two of them were alive.

And then the cook reappeared and grabbed on to the canister. But just as quickly as Jessica Black had arrived, a huge wave snatched her away again.

Now Jones told Scornavacchi that he had seen lights underwater, near where the ship was. They thought of returning to the ship to see if the lights meant other survivors. They abandoned the idea, however, because they could barely hold on to the canister, which they were still struggling to open.

As they fought to open the canister, an inflated life raft floated toward the two men. They swam to it and found Warner and Sprague already holding on to the raft.

Individually, the four each tried twice to climb into the raft. But the opening was too high. In the survival suits, every movement was difficult, draining all their strength.

It was while they were clinging to the raft that Sprague

heard, from the direction of the ship, the voice of a woman calling.

"Help me! I'm caught," the voice pleaded. Sprague didn't know who it was. But the ship was far away. There was no way to get to it, she thought.

Instead, Sprague and her crewmates around the raft thought hard about how they could climb inside. Someone suggested Sprague might be the lightest. If the three men could push her high enough, perhaps she could crawl into the raft's door. It took time, but it worked, and she made it inside.

Sprague now pulled Warner's harness and, although his immersion suit was weighed down by seawater, he clambered into the raft. The two inside the raft hauled Scornavacchi inside.

While they were bringing Jones aboard, Scornavacchi crossed the raft and looked out the second small doorway. There he found Sanders, Faunt, and Black clinging to the side. The work was slow. It took half an hour, but the three other survivors were hauled in, too. In the end, there were seven aboard this twenty-five-person raft, sprawled across the floor.

But they knew they were not yet safe. Each wondered about the other nine crew members. Through the open door, they could see *Bounty*. They were being driven away from their ship, and they saw no one else in the water. Were they alone?

"Do you think everybody made it?" Someone in the raft asked the question they all were thinking.

"Yep," Sanders said. "They all made it." But he didn't know for sure.

Scornavacchi and Sprague now asked everybody to hold hands while they prayed. Then they asked if anyone else wanted to pray with them.

"I don't have faith in God," Faunt said, "but I have faith in the coast guard."

Now Scornavacchi began singing a song about going home, one the crew had sung in every port.

The sailors would sing and then pray, but the ride was less than peaceful. Suddenly, a huge wave hit the raft, and it folded like a taco, throwing the seven into a heap on one side. The silence they had experienced in the troughs was gone. Back atop the waves, the sea was loud, violent.

Once a wave passed, the raft would unfold as the sailors spread themselves around and resumed casual conversations laced with jokes.

Bang! They were folded into a taco again.

They quickly adjusted to this new maritime routine. Fold, flatten, resume talking, as if nothing had happened.

And every once in a while, over the raft noise, they would hear their hope in a sound from above: the drone of a C-130.

CHAPTER 15

The Second Raft

Third Mate Dan Cleveland was near the Nav Shack companionway when he heard John Svendsen tell Robin Walbridge that the bow had gone underwater. Cleveland could not then have imagined how he and his girlfriend, Laura Groves, would find the same haven. But they did.

When the ship capsized, he saw his crewmates, who had been making their way aft toward the life rafts, tossed about, assaulted by loose or broken parts of the ship. Then Cleveland found himself floating in warm water. His gloved hands grabbed something—a wooden grating— and he started kicking his feet to get away from the ship.

Moments passed as he struggled against the sea, and

then he found Groves. There seemed to be a current that was taking them together forward along the side of the rolling ship. The current pulled them toward the main and fore masts. The masts, along with their miles of rope rigging, rose up out of the water, only to come slashing back into the sea, lethal clubs threatening to pummel the swimmers.

Groves had been struggling to keep her face out of the water when, in the moonlight, something—she didn't know what—struck her on the head. Time lost its meaning. There was only survival. And then there was Cleveland, clinging to the wooden grating to help keep her afloat.

Adam Prokosh, incapacitated earlier, had made it to the weather deck and then back to the stern, near the life rafts. When the deck reared to vertical, he let himself slide down to the helm. Then, injured or not, he jumped.

A mast rose, streaming seawater from its rigging, then like a tree felled by a logger, crashed back into the sea. Prokosh escaped being hit by the mast, but a wooden grating hit him in the head. Then a yard on the mast slammed him. He was driven under the surface but managed, even with painful back injuries, to swim up. When he broke the surface, he found fellow crew members nearby.

Jessica Hewitt had been near the helm. She had chosen not to wear a life jacket. She didn't want to be encumbered. But she and her boyfriend, Drew Salapatek, had connected their harnesses, which someone had suggested. She thought that in those winds and seas, she would rather be clipped on to someone than holding their hand for safety. But then she was in the water and she was connected to no one.

When she and Salapatek were thrown into the water, Salapatek felt they were being held underwater. They seemed to be snagged, perhaps by their harnesses and tethers. He was being held under the waves, and his first reaction was to rid himself of his harness—losing the connection to Hewitt in the process. Still submerged, he curled his legs up and shoved the harness off with his hands.

Once he surfaced, Salapatek was alone in the water for a short time before he saw a group of immersion suits. He swam toward them, finding Hewitt and Groves and Cleveland. The three were clinging to the wooden grating when he joined them.

Sometime later, Prokosh and Barksdale joined these four. Then, next to *Bounty*'s hull, someone in the group spotted an inflated life raft. No one on board had deployed any of the rafts, so this one had to have been set free by its hydrostatic (water-activated) release when the deck had gone underwater. The raft floated toward them, and the six swam to it. But the wind that drove the raft moved it beyond their reach.

Soon, they saw a life raft canister floating nearby. Cleveland had tied a long rope to the cannister earlier, and Barksdale found the rope and let the canister float away a distance before he yanked on it. The yanking triggered a CO_2 cartridge inside the canister, opening it and inflating the raft. What emerged was a twenty-five-person raft. It was thirteen feet in diameter with black rubber tubing and an orange canopy.

The gloves of the immersion suits were stiff, making it difficult for Barksdale to hold on to the rope, called a painter. Cleveland also grabbed the painter, wrapping it around his fist. Then the rest of the swimmers joined in to form a chain, hauling on the line, drawing themselves closer to the raft.

Catching the life raft was exhausting. The swimmers wanted to take a break before climbing in, but they found there was no easy way to hold on. There was a line for that purpose circling the raft, but the clumsy immersion suit gloves made grabbing it impossible.

Groves got an idea and bit the line, pulling it with her teeth away from the inflated tubing far enough to slide her gloved hand up under the line. Then she hooked her forearm over the line and hung there, trying to relax, recover.

Climbing into a life raft might be easy in a swimming pool during training, as several of the crew members had done. Hewitt saw that in thirty-foot seas, this would be a challenge. But she noticed that everyone around her appeared to be calm. And she realized that she was not afraid. She felt safe in her immersion suit, floating beside the life raft far from shore at the edge of a passing hurricane.

Prokosh, injured and in pain, clipped the tether from his harness to the line encircling the raft. Then he lay on his back, trying to conserve energy. The waves pushed him to the end of the ten-foot tether, a short distance from the others.

Groves was the first to attempt to enter the raft, and she discovered a new issue. Her immersion suit had filled with water. There was too much wet ballast in the legs of her suit, making her too heavy to climb aboard. Every other effort by the six to enter the raft failed until Salapatek managed to get his knee onto Cleveland's thigh. It was just enough of a lift to get Salapatek's belly on top of the raft tube. He, too, had water in his survival suit legs, but with Cleveland and the others shoving from below, he was able to squirm on his stomach and get his torso into the raft.

Salapatek helped haul Cleveland aboard, and together, they got Prokosh and the three others inside. Prokosh endured more pain being pulled into the raft, but there was no other choice. They were riding up the faces of still monstrous seas and sliding down the wave backs, but they were contained inside the raft.

There were emergency supplies inside, as well as a lot of seawater. Hampered by the immersion suit gloves, the crew couldn't open the supplies, so Cleveland stripped down the top of his suit and, with his hands free, opened the supplies. The crew now began looking for a container to bail out water but found none. They spread out to distribute their weight evenly and then opened the water bottles contained with the other supplies. When his bottle was empty, Cleveland started bailing with it. Although the seawater was warm, the third mate noticed that he was getting cold, so he pulled the top of his suit back on.

Occasionally, breaking waves would splash through the raft's opening. Although they tried, the crew members couldn't find a way to zip the opening shut.

They just had to stay alive and hope a helicopter would come to them.

John Svendsen was adrift on the dark ocean all alone. After he shouted that the crew was abandoning ship into the radio, a torrent of water pummeled him down onto the steps of the companionway. He fought his way against the torrent and escaped to the weather deck. There he saw Walbridge climbing out along a horizontal mast before he jumped in the water.

In all of this, Svendsen had suffered numerous injuries—his face was battered, he had wounds on his head and neck, broken bones in his right hand, and trauma to his chest and abdomen.

In the water, he did not hear or see other crew members. He found an unopened life raft canister, which he could not open and so abandoned it. Later, Svendsen found a strobe light, which flashed in the dark, and kept it with him. Buoyed by his immersion suit, his distinctive long hair hidden inside the featureless hood, he floated, like a piece of debris. He could see empty immersion suits among the timbers and gratings and rigging and, not that far away, the still-floating wreck of *Bounty*.

Slowly, the first mate drifted away from the ship, a solitary speck on the ocean.

CHAPTER 16

"Are the Sailors Alive?"

MONDAY, EARLY MORNING, OCTOBER 29

Peering out the rain-streaked aircraft windshield, Wes McIntosh gazed at *Bounty*'s rafts, and he noticed something that gave him a glimmer of hope. The two rafts from *Bounty* were not tumbling, and he thought maybe that was because there were people inside.

Fuel was running low and although McIntosh knew another C-130 would soon launch, he wasn't sure he could stay on scene until they arrived. Over the headset, he instructed the drop-master to release a self-locating data-marker buoy. This would electronically mark *Bounty*'s position for the other aircrews.

Mike Myers was on the radio with Sector, and he

turned to McIntosh and said, "The other C-130 has already launched, and a Jayhawk helicopter will launch in a couple minutes."

For the first time since they arrived at the distress scene, McIntosh felt relief wash over him. It would be daylight soon, and if the *Bounty* sailors were still alive, these additional resources would find them and begin a rescue.

During the next half hour, the C-130 alternated between flying at seven thousand feet for less turbulence and better communication with Sector, and then dropping down to five hundred feet to search for survivors. The crew could see several blinking strobe lights. They realized the strobes were attached to survival suits, but it was impossible to tell if anyone was in the suits.

It was still dark when the second C-130, flown by Commander Peyton Russell, neared the search scene. Russell was flying with copilot Aaron Cmiel, flight mechanic Corey Lupton, MSOs David Dull and Lee Christensen, drop-master Jonathan Sageser, and basic air crewman Austin Black.

While in route, Russell was briefed on the radio by McIntosh and Myers. They described how *Bounty*'s first mate had abruptly shouted, "We are abandoning ship!"

how the vessel capsized, and that they didn't know for sure where the survivors were.

A few minutes later, the second C-130 arrived, and Commander Russell took over as on-scene coordinator. He immediately began searching the water for signs of life.

Drop-master Sageser, using his night-vision goggles, surveyed the debris field. He couldn't shake the feeling that he was looking down inside a giant washing machine. Sageser had done more than his share of search and rescues, but he had never seen waves so confused, coming from all directions. The crashing waves looked like endless miles of white-capped mountains. *It's going to be tough to spot anyone in the water*, he thought. *That helo can't get here soon enough. They can hover and get a better look at each of the strobes.*

In need of fuel, McIntosh headed toward Raleigh, making one last pass over the life rafts and then over *Bounty*, where he saw a strange and haunting site. Up until this point the vessel had been laying on its side, its masts battering the ocean's surface into a froth as waves made them rise and fall. Now the masts were straight up, pointing toward the C-130, as if the ship were coming back to life.

McIntosh shook his head, wondering if the plane's wild vacillations were making his eyes play tricks on him. Then he realized what had happened. As the interior of the ship filled with additional water, it spread out more evenly. That caused the ship to right itself, even though the deck was now several feet under water.

The MSOs used a night-vision camera that allowed them to zoom in for a better look, and they had the clearest view. One empty survival suit with a blinking strobe was caught in a mast. All three of the *Bounty*'s masts had their top few feet shorn away, but the rigging and shroud lines were still attached to the masts and the yardarms. The lines ran down from the masts and disappeared into the ocean, where they were swallowed up by the foaming white sea, giving the impression that the ship was poking up through clouds.

Not an inch of the deck could be seen. But because the masts and lines were still intact, *Bounty* had the look of a ghost ship that could rise up and sail yet again.

McIntosh then steered the plane toward the coast. *Are the sailors alive?* he wondered. *If they were in the life rafts, why didn't they fire a flare?* He tried to push a disturbing thought out of his mind. *Did we just witness the death of sixteen people?*

PART III

CHAPTER 17

Helicopter Pilot
Steve Cerveny

MONDAY, EARLY MORNING, OCTOBER 29

Lieutenant Commander Steve Cerveny had had a long night. The Jayhawk helicopter pilot began his day at Air Station Elizabeth City at 8:00 a.m. Sunday morning as the "ready" aircraft commander if he was called upon to fly. It was a quiet day up until Sector notified him of *Bounty*'s problems in the evening. He and Duty Officer Todd Farrell immediately learned all they could about the vessel and its predicament.

The slim, forty-three-year-old pilot, with a touch of gray in his hair, had more than twenty years of flying time. He sensed that *Bounty* might be in bigger trouble than its captain realized. After all, the ship was in the path of a hurricane that Cerveny had heard meteorologists begin referring to as "mammoth" and a "Frankenstorm."

Cerveny's career as a helicopter pilot began in the navy when he started flight school in 1992. After almost ten years flying for the navy, he transitioned to the coast guard. There he began flying the HH-60 Jayhawk, a twenty-thousand-pound, sixty-five-foot-long helicopter, used for long-range rescues.

Cerveny had been one of the pilots who flew multiple rescues over several days when Hurricane Katrina hit New Orleans in 2005. Then, in 2010, Cerveny was the one who needed to be rescued, after an awful crash onboard a Jayhawk. He had been the aircraft's copilot and was traveling over a remote, mountainous region of Utah after providing security for the Winter Olympics in Vancouver, British Columbia.

Snow had been falling during the flight and some was sticking to the aircraft, forcing the pilots to activate the engine anti-icing mechanism. As they increased altitude over higher terrain, another coast guard helicopter flying in tandem with Cerveny's disappeared into a cloud bank. Somewhere in front of both aircrafts was a ridgeline that the pilots knew they must fly over.

The commander had been flying the helicopter from the left seat, and Cerveny was in the right. As the commander tried to gain additional altitude to crest the ten-thousand-foot ridgeline, the Jayhawk was not responding. Cerveny called for more airspeed, realizing the anti-icing mechanism was robbing them of power. But the aircraft was sluggish, and the commander had no choice except to turn away from the mountaintops.

Banking hard to the right, both men were horrified to see treetops emerge from the clouds just a few feet in front of them. The rotors clipped the trees, and in a split second, the giant steel bird lurched to a stop. Then it plummeted sideways, crashing through pines and into the snow.

When the helicopter finally came to rest, Cerveny felt a searing pain shooting through his leg. He looked for the commander who should have been in the seat to his left. Instead he saw snow. Cerveny released his safety harness and tried to stand. That's when he noticed the lower part of his leg was turned inward at a 45-degree angle and blood was seeping through his pants.

The commander's head popped out of the snow, but he too was injured. Both men were trapped in the steaming, hissing aircraft that could ignite at any moment. In the rear of the helicopter, basic air crew member Gina Panuzzi was critically hurt with severe internal injuries. Luckily, rescue swimmer Darren Hicks and flight mechanic Edward Sychra were relatively unscathed. They started pulling the injured from the wreckage, which was scattered over hundreds of feet, including up in the trees.

The accident had happened so quickly that no emergency call could be made. The lead helicopter pilots that had been in front of Cerveny's aircraft didn't know they had gone down. Now, the five survivors were fighting against the clock; their injuries and hypothermia would sap their strength and soon snuff out their lives.

Flight mechanic Sychra used his cell phone to send a text message to the flight mechanic of the lead helicopter, who texted back that they were alerting authorities and were going to land as close to the crash site as possible.

In the meantime, Cerveny's open compound fracture was causing excruciating pain, and the rescue swimmer, Hicks, did his best to help by using a tree branch as a splint. Cerveny thought to himself, *Well, I'm responsible for getting us into this jam, and maybe now God is going to help us get out of it.* Despite the pain, he felt a calmness come over him, and his thoughts turned to the more seriously injured Gina Panuzzi. He knew she needed medical attention immediately.

A short time later, the lead helicopter returned, but the Jayhawk was incapable of hovering at that altitude. Pilot Steven Bonn flew to a lower altitude and lightened the aircraft by dumping fuel and equipment. Then he returned, and, in an amazing display of skill, somehow guided the helicopter down into a confined opening in the woods, just a couple hundred yards below the crash site.

A MedFlight helicopter also landed nearby, and the injured were whisked off to Salt Lake City. Snowmobilers arrived on scene, and they took Sychra and rescue swimmer Hicks down off the mountain.

Though Steve Cerveny survived, his leg was mangled. He had surgery, but afterward his orthopedic doctor warned him that the damage was so serious he could still lose the limb. But after two more surgeries and a month in the hospital, the leg was saved. Yet he was given the bitter news that he may not be able to ever put weight on his leg and his flying days were likely over.

For the next several months, Cerveny directed his energy into physical therapy, and with each step, he began to realize he might someday fly again. Approximately a year and a half after the accident, in October 2011, Cerveny was behind the controls of a Jayhawk again, and throttled the helicopter off the tarmac and into the sky.

Early on October 29, Cerveny had been lying awake, wondering what was happening aboard the tall ship *Bounty*. He didn't have to speculate for long. At 3:00 a.m. Todd Farrell called and asked him to come into the Operations Center.

Copilot Jane Pena had also been alerted, and all three reviewed the situation with Sector. At that point, the *Bounty* had not yet capsized, but just a short time later Sector called and relayed the urgent message from McIntosh that people on the *Bounty* were abandoning ship at that very moment. That call changed everything. There was no time to wait for safer conditions at dawn.

The search and rescue alarm sounded its whooping warble. Rescue swimmer Randy Haba and flight mechanic Michael Lufkin ran to the Operations Center to join up with Cerveny and Pena. Cerveny explained what was happening with the *Bounty*, and then described the extreme conditions at the accident scene. He asked each crew member if they felt alert enough to execute the mission, knowing that all of them were near the end of their twenty-four-hour shift. They responded affirmatively and raced to the helicopter that was already out of the hangar, fueled and ready to go.

CHAPTER 18

One Small Strobe Light All Alone

MONDAY, EARLY MORNING, OCTOBER 29

Michael Lufkin and Jane Pena had done only a couple helicopter rescues and were glad to have been paired with veterans like Haba and Cerveny. Lufkin, a tall and lanky twenty-five-year-old, had been in the coast guard for five years, serving in different roles. He had been a qualified flight mechanic for only seven months, and it would be his job to raise and lower the cable and help guide the pilots during the hoists. The cable is a key piece of equipment for rescue: The rescue swimmer will hook himself to the cable via his harness, and the cable will lower him to the ocean and also bring him back up to the helicopter.

Randy Haba's life would literally be in Lufkin's hands, because Lufkin, not Haba, controlled the movements of the cable when the rescue swimmer was on the other end. Once Haba was in the ocean, he would then be the one putting survivors in the rescue basket for Lufkin to hoist up to the helicopter. Lufkin would need to factor in the wind and waves to get the swimmer in the sweet spot of the back side of a wave, with just enough slack in the cable to allow the swimmer to maneuver. He would want to avoid putting Haba in the middle of a breaking wave, where he could get buried.

Now, as Lufkin sat in the helicopter's cabin during lift-off into the darkness, all the various hoisting scenarios were going through his mind. He would need to combine quickness and strength in many of the hoisting proce-dures. Those skills were necessary when dropping the swimmer into the sea, bringing the hook up and attaching the basket, and getting survivors into the helo as quickly as possible.

Fortunately, Lufkin was a natural athlete, and the coor-dination required would not be a problem. Still, he had never flown into weather anything remotely like Hurri-cane Sandy. One thing was for certain: He knew he didn't want his swimmer or the basket anywhere near the ship's masts. Should the cable become entangled in the rigging, it could pull the giant helo right out of the sky.

The pilots flew at an altitude of three thousand feet, using a strong tail wind to propel them at one hundred seventy knots. Off Cape Hatteras, they slowly descended and reduced speed. Cerveny ordered his crew to "goggle up" and don the night-vision goggles so they could see the water, which came into focus at about three hundred feet in altitude.

Squalls of rain and wind gusts began rocking the Jayhawk. A couple powerful gusts made the helo rise and fall unexpectedly by as much as fifty feet. The on-scene C-130 pilot, Peyton Russell, kept the Jayhawk crew updated through their headsets. They knew conditions would deteriorate with each passing mile.

Michael Lufkin paid particular attention to the talk about the many strobe lights blinking in the water. He knew there was going to be searching involved, and fuel could become an issue, making quick hoists imperative. Lufkin reckoned that not only would a second helo be needed immediately, but most likely a third—there could be sixteen potential survivors scattered around the capsized *Bounty*.

Jane Pena, who sat in the left cockpit seat, had already

started making fuel calculations. She needed to establish their "bingo" time: the moment they absolutely must leave the accident scene to ensure enough fuel was left to make it back to land.

The thirty-one-year-old copilot with short brown hair had been a bit on edge when they were flying at three thousand feet in the pitch dark. But now that she could see the ocean through her night-vision goggles, she felt fine. Water was her element, and just seeing it had a calming effect. Like Michael Lufkin, this was her first major SAR case. She knew she would be learning from one of the top pilots in Steve Cerveny, and felt glad for the opportunity. *This is what all those hours of training and studying were for*, she thought, remembering her long and difficult quest to become a pilot.

Pena grew up in Washington State and was a born athlete, climbing trees, camping, hiking, and playing soccer and baseball. She had always wanted to fly, but instead ended up joining the coast guard in 2007. Her first position involved offshore security boardings of foreign vessels, a job she really loved. But she hadn't given up on flying and kept applying for flight school until she was finally selected. Graduating or "winged" in March of 2010, Pena's first air station was Elizabeth City. And now, she was about to see why the ocean off Cape Hatteras is called the Graveyard of the Atlantic.

◀▬▶

It took about an hour for the helicopter to reach *Bounty*. In the C-130, Peyton Russell was on the radio, telling Pena that he had passed over one particular strobe and survival suit that did not float like the others. "We've marked the location, and we think there might be a person in that suit."

Pena and Cerveny understood this was the target they needed to go to first. Unlike the large rafts, this single strobe light, far from *Bounty*, could be easy to lose sight of in the waves. And should the strobe light's batteries die out, they might never find that potential survivor.

Cerveny guided the helo to the coordinates Pena relayed to him, a full three-quarters of a mile away from the ship and rafts. As they descended toward the lone strobe light, Pena got her first closeup view of the ocean, and it looked crazed.

"Normally," recalled Pena, "waves would be advancing from a single direction, and there would be a set amount of space between each one. These waves, however, had nothing normal about them." They were coming from various directions, with no pattern to them. Sometimes the waves slammed into one another shooting spray into the dark sky.

The pilots had a good view of the chaos below: Besides the windows directly in front of the cockpit, there were small windows at foot level and on the sides. In the cabin, Haba and Lufkin peered out small windows on either side of the aircraft. They too were in awe of the unusual waves, varying in size from twenty-five to thirty feet.

Winds made hovering in place nearly impossible, and Cerveny did his best to hold the iron bird in position over the single strobe light. The crew could see the outline of the immersion suit, but there was no sign of life. To get lower, Cerveny let the wind blow the helo back a bit and then he angled the nose down, descending to sixty feet.

Pena watched the radar altimeter, an instrument that shows exactly how much distance there is between the aircraft and the ocean. It fluctuated between twenty-five and sixty feet, meaning that when a large wave passed beneath the helicopter it was only twenty-five feet from them.

Pena wanted to make sure they never got any closer than twenty-five feet. She focused on scanning the seas to make sure there weren't any extreme or "rogue" waves coming their way. Even if the wave itself didn't hit the helicopter, its spray could be ingested by the engine and cause "flame out." If that happened, the Jayhawk would stall and drop like a stone. (Should a helo hit the water, its heavy rotors, extending fifty-four feet in diameter, would pull it upside down.) The crew trained for this dire scenario, but successfully exiting the aircraft at night in thirty-foot seas would be a long shot. With that in mind, Pena only glanced at the survival suit, instead keeping her eyes peeled for an extreme wave that could kill them all.

Lufkin removed his goggles in preparation to do a hoist if necessary. Suddenly, over his headset, he heard Cerveny say, "I just saw the arm of the survival suit lift out of the water! We've got a person down there." A shot of adrenaline coursed through Lufkin, and he looked at Haba. They were officially out of the search mode and into a rescue.

Bounty under sail was a handsome ship. [Scott Maguire]

A view of
Bounty's deck
[McNealy]

The Great Cabin belowdecks at the stern [McNealy]

Captain Robin
Walbridge
[B. Neff]

audene Christian
as a relatively
w crew member.
[Neff]

Doug Faunt was
the most senior
crew member.
[Doug Faunt]

Bounty in rough seas on a prior trip [Marc Castells]

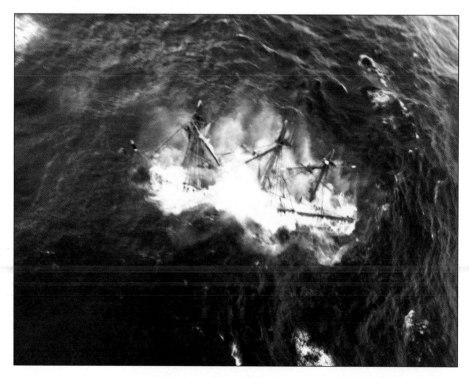

Hurricane Sandy knocked Bounty on her side. [Tim Kuklewski]

A third Coast Guard helicopter found *Bounty*
in this position later in the morning. [Tim Kuklewski]

C-130 pilot Wes McIntosh receiving an award
for his assistance in the rescue. [U.S. Coast Guard]

The second helicopter crew (left to right) Daniel Todd, Jenny Fields, Steve Bonn, and Neil Moulder [U.S. Coast Guard]

Rescue swimmer at life raft [Brandyn Hill]

Survivor being taken from helicopter [U.S. Coast Guard]

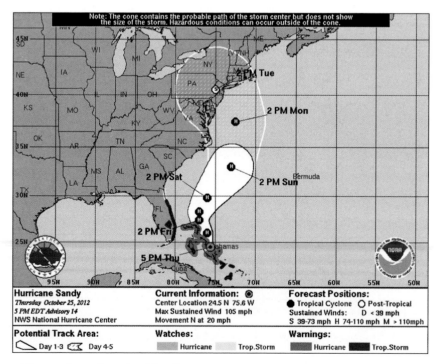

The projected path of Sandy [National Weather Service]

CHAPTER 19

A Swirling Vortex

MONDAY, EARLY MORNING, OCTOBER 29

Randy Haba had taken off his helmet with the radio set and exchanged it for a neon-green rescue helmet. Now he was donning his harness, flippers, mask, and snorkel. A determined look was on his face. The rescue swimmer wore a dry suit, which unlike a wet suit did not allow any water inside and would protect Haba from hypothermia. But Haba knew it would make him sweat profusely in the warmer waters of the Gulf Stream, but he was not complaining. Should disaster happen—and he couldn't get back into the helicopter—the extra layer of protection just might save his life.

He slid toward the open doorway. With the illumination

from the helicopter's searchlight, he could see the person's head and arm sticking out of the ocean. Earlier, Haba had used the aircraft's infrared camera, which could help in the search for survivors by showing a person's body heat as white against a green background on the monitor. The lens of the camera was mounted in the nose of the helicopter, and Haba used a toggle to move it, while zooming in and out, and adjust for focusing.

Haba had seen a bit of white coming from the survival suit. He figured there was someone alive in it, and he prepared for deployment. Wanting to do the hoist as quickly as possible, he told Lufkin he thought a direct deployment—where the swimmer stays on the hook and brings the survivor up with him in a sling—would be the way to go.

Haba felt a mixture of excitement and tension, the same kind an athlete might get before the start of a big game. He always thought that if the day ever came and he didn't get that amped-up feeling before a rescue, he should resign from being a rescue swimmer. That's when mistakes are made, as soon as you get complacent.

Haba, at thirty-three years of age, was a powerful, muscular man, standing at six foot one and weighing close to two hundred pounds. Like all rescue swimmers he was paid to stay in top shape. His background would not, however, suggest that he was destined to become a rescue swimmer. The first few years of his life had been spent on the family farm in Nebraska, and then later in the farming town of Stratton, Colorado. He loved sports, especially football, and his high school team had won numerous state titles. But he was not on the swim team, nor had he been an especially strong swimmer.

It was a high school science teacher who had introduced him to the possibility of a career in the outdoors, particularly search and rescue. Later, in college, when a coast guard recruiter showed him a video of a helicopter rescue swimmer, Haba was instantly hooked—despite the fact that he had never even seen the ocean.

During coast guard boot camp, despite not being as quick a swimmer as some of the other candidates, he was determined, and completed the four-month program. Then it was on to Air Station Elizabeth City for the more grueling Aviation Survival Technician "A" School, where he quickly became a stronger swimmer. About half the trainees washed out of the program, but the football player in Haba wouldn't consider quitting. He pushed himself both physically and mentally in ways he had never done before.

After graduating, he was transferred back to New Orleans and flew on more than one hundred fifty search-and-rescue cases during the next four years. A stint in Puerto Rico followed, and then it was back to Elizabeth City, where he became a rescue swimmer instructor. Now it was Haba who was sizing up candidates. He knew the best swimmers were not necessarily the fastest ones, but those who were the most committed and showed it through endurance and dedication.

After instructing for a couple of years, Haba was picked for a program that allowed him to continue college, and during that time, he also got married. The coast guard life had been good to Haba, and now he was going to earn his pay by putting his life on the line for total strangers.

Crouched by the open cabin doorway of the Jayhawk, Haba squinted through the wind-blown rain. He looked down to where the helicopter's spotlight illuminated the survivor being shoved around by waves. The rescue swimmer was trying to get a feel for the way the waves were washing under the survivor. He realized these were some of the most confused seas he'd ever seen. He suspected there was a strong current from the Gulf Stream, and he mentally prepared himself to fight both that and the towering seas.

The roar from the wind mixing with that of the rotors made it nearly impossible for Haba to talk with hoist operator Lufkin. They shouted about how they would do this rescue. Haba clipped the cable to his harness and had the sling or "strop" also clipped to his harness. If the rescue went as planned, Haba would first be lowered to the survivor. Then he'd get the survivor in the strop, and they'd come up together. Haba's legs would be wrapped around the survivor to make sure they didn't slip out of the sling.

Lufkin was in a kneeling position by the cabin door. He wore a gunner's belt around his waist that extended to a secure point on the opposite cabin wall to keep him from falling out the door should he slip. One leather-gloved hand gripped the cable. His other hand held a pendant attached to a long wire cord that controlled the hoist.

The cable was suspended from a steel arm extending from the airframe above the door. It is composed of woven steel strands and is only about 3/8 of an inch in diameter, yet strong enough to hoist 11,000 pounds. The dozens of individual strands give the cable its durability and strength, but they also present a weakness. Individual strands have been known to break by rubbing against the aircraft or another object. Although this doesn't usually mean the cable will break, it can lead to fouling or "bird caging" in the spool.

Should the cable become stuck while the rescue swimmer is in the water, the stranded swimmer would be in as much danger as the survivors, and perhaps more if he is unable to reach the life raft.

◣▬▬▬▶

Cerveny positioned the aircraft in a holding hover just a bit aft of the survivor. The rotor wash kicked up foam and thick bands of spray, making it look like the survivor was in the middle of a tornado.

While the commander was working the levers that controlled the helicopters movements, Pena continually scanned the ocean. So far, no rogue waves had materialized, but every now and then she'd give an alert such as "Larger one coming from the left." Then Cerveny would increase altitude slightly to keep that cushion of twenty-five feet above the tallest of waves.

In the cabin, Lufkin spoke through the radio in his headset.

"Swimmer is ready and at the door."

Cerveny acknowledged and gave the okay for deployment.

Lufkin tried to stay as calm as possible. He would now be doing two things at once: lowering the swimmer while "conning" (instructing) the pilots with directions for exactly where he wanted them to move the aircraft. His words must be precise because the pilots would be scanning their instruments and the seas around them—but unable to see the rescue swimmer much of the time.

Lufkin tapped Haba on the chest, the signal that he was ready. The swimmer responded with a thumbs-up sign.

"Deploying the swimmer," said Lufkin.

Haba pushed off, and Lufkin started lowering him, saying "Swimmer is outside the cabin. Swimmer is being lowered."

Lufkin now knew just how strong the winds were. Haba went sailing aft of the aircraft, and Lufkin had to crane his neck just to keep him in sight.

Down went Haba, making contact with the water about forty feet behind the survivor. He immediately started swimming, but a wave dropped out from under him, and the cable violently jerked him back twenty feet, almost ripping his mask off. The next wave blindsided him, crushing into his back while in an awkward position.

So much adrenaline was surging through Haba that he didn't feel any pain despite the fact that later X-rays revealed a compressed vertebra with a hairline fracture. In the water, he was more mad than anything else. He cursed to himself, realizing they'd lost valuable time.

Lufkin did the same as he worked the cable. He lifted Haba out of the water before another wave could slam into him. Over his headset, he explained to the pilots what had happened. Then he said he was repositioning the swimmer, telling them to ease the aircraft "forward, ten feet."

Hanging at the end of the cable, Haba knew how hard it must be for Lufkin to time his descent in such conditions. The wind was so strong, it felt like the swimmer was sticking his head out of a speeding car.

"I couldn't wear my night-vision goggles," recalled Lufkin, "and do the hoist at the same time. So I had to rely on the fixed spotlight shining directly downward, which only gave me a small viewing area. Waves would appear out of the dark from different directions. I had to make a split decision when to lower the swimmer again. When I saw what looked like a lull after a wave had passed, I pressed the pendant and Haba was back in the water."

This time Haba was within a few feet of the survivor. Then suddenly, a wind gust pushed the helicopter upward, causing the swimmer to be jerked beyond reach of the drifting mariner.

Haba gave Lufkin the thumbs-down sign to indicate he'd need more slack in the cable to combat the unexpected gusts.

On the third attempt, the rescue swimmer finally reached the survivor. Haba could see that it was a man, still conscious but quite pale and exhausted looking.

Haba removed his snorkel and shouted, "Are you hurt?"

"I'm okay," croaked the man.

"Is there anyone else in the water nearby?"

"Don't think so."

Haba was relieved to see that the man was not only coherent but calm. Far too often, swimmers have to subdue panicked survivors who, instead of following the rescuer's direction, claw or fight them.

"Okay, here's what we're going to do!" shouted Haba, holding on to the survivor's arm. Before he could explain, a breaking sea avalanched on the two men like a pile driver. It pushed them downward, into a swirling vortex.

CHAPTER 20

"Like We've Flown Back in Time"

SUNDAY, APPROXIMATELY 5:00 A.M. TO 6:00 A.M., OCTOBER 29

Lufkin held his breath, searching for the men in the foam. Over his headset he conned the pilots. It was next to impossible to hover in the same place with the varying wind gusts. He directed their movement based on where he thought he sighted the Haba and the *Bounty* survivor below.

"Left, ten feet," said Lufkin. "Okay, now forward fifteen."

The neon rescue helmet appeared directly below Lufkin. It was one of the best sights he'd ever seen.

Below, Haba took a gulp of air. He put the strop around the survivor, worried another wave would cause him to become separated from the man in the dark. He cinched the strop up tight and hollered, "We're going up together! Keep your arms down on the sling. I don't want you falling out!"

Haba looked up toward the helo thundering overhead and gave the signal that they were ready to be retrieved. Lufkin started retracting the cable. Soon the two men on the other end left the waves. They were greeted by the howling wind, blowing them aft of the helo, spinning them in the process.

Using his gloved hand, Lufkin, laying on his belly, held the cable as steady as he could. His big fear was that the cable could swing so far aft, it would become jammed behind the open door. He kept retracting cable, and soon the men were at the door. Leaning out of the aircraft, Lufkin grabbed Haba's harness and used all his strength to pull the two men safely inside.

In the back of his mind, Lufkin wondered why the two men felt like the weight of three. He had his answer by just looking at the survivor's immersion suit, where the water had collected in the feet and legs. *That thing must have a hundred pounds of water in it*, Lufkin thought to himself. Then he moved to the door, continued updating the pilots as he had been all along. With a sigh of relief he finally said, "Swimmer and survivor safely in the cabin. Door is now closed."

The survivor was John Svendsen.

The C-130 flown by Mike Myers and Wes McIntosh was almost back to Raleigh. Over the radio, Sector informed them that the first survivor had been successfully hoisted. Roars of applause and cheering erupted on the plane. "It was utter elation," recalled Myers. "Our hearts had remained with the crew of the *Bounty*. It was beyond nerve-racking to not know if they went down with the ship. But when we heard that helicopter crew had just arrived and already plucked one out of the sea, that gave us hope for the rest of them."

Once McIntosh and Myers had safely landed and refueled the plane, they entered the airport's flight planning room. Someone asked, "Were you the guys out there with the *Bounty*?" Myers and McIntosh were taken aback, they were used to flying in anonymity, with no one outside the coast guard knowing what they did.

Myers answered, "Yes, that was us. But how did you know?" The person pointed up at a television set. On it was a photo of the *Bounty*, and a reporter was saying how the ship had sunk in the hurricane. Both C-130 pilots knew this case was turning out to be unlike any other. They stayed glued to the television set, waiting to see if there was more news of survivors, prepared to fly again if needed.

◣▬▬◢

The faint light of dawn filtered through the rain and clouds, and Steve Cerveny guided the helicopter into a wide turn, heading toward *Bounty*. On the way, the crew saw another couple of lone strobe lights. They hovered over them with the searchlight, trying to determine if the survival suits were empty. When they arrived at the masted ship, Pena thought, *This is surreal. It's like we've flown back in time.*

Randy Haba had a similar reaction: He had seen many foundering vessels, but never a tall ship with three enormous masts. He hoped he would not have to be lowered to the ship, noting the tangled rigging fanning out from the vessel.

A blinking strobe light in one of the masts caught the attention of the aircrew. Cerveny lowered the helo down to forty feet for a better look. Within seconds, it was clear that the strobe was on an empty survival suit. The aircrew continued scanning the ship and the surrounding wreckage for survivors. As they fanned out into ever wider circles, they saw another empty survival suit but no people.

Five minutes later, Pena radioed the C-130. "We've searched the ship and the surrounding debris, and there are no survivors."

The pilots on the C-130 acknowledged, and then guided the helicopter to the nearest life raft, which was about a mile away. The raft's orange canopy was not inflated, and there was no one on top of it or under it.

Pena started getting worried. *Where are they? Surely there has to be more than one person alive.* They hovered over the raft, hoping a head or arm would pop out from beneath the canopy.

"No survivors in the raft we are over," said Pena to the C-130. "It is one of our coast guard rafts."

"Roger. The other three rafts are lined up in almost a straight line to the east. They are about a mile apart."

"Okay," said Pena, "we are proceeding to the next one."

This raft was also a coast guard raft. Again, they hovered over the raft, and again, there were no signs of life. *This is bad,* thought Pena. *There were sixteen people on this ship. They can't all be gone.*

CHAPTER 21

"Are You Ready to Go?"

The Jayhawk moved on to the next raft. This one had a red canopy, fully inflated. Cerveny put the helo in a hover, slowly descending to thirty feet above the seas. The raft looked stable, and he took that to be a good sign: Maybe there were people inside weighing it down. But there was no sign of life below, and he thought, *Please, not another empty life raft. Somebody else has to be alive.*

A second later, a head popped out of the doorway and a survivor started waving. All four aircrew members breathed a collective sigh of relief.

Haba had decided against staying attached to the hook for the next rescue. Instead, he would do a harness deployment where he would detach from the cable and swim to the raft. Michael Lufkin relayed this to the pilots, got the okay from Cerveny, and then began the process of putting Haba in the water.

When the swimmer hit the water, about forty feet from the raft, he unhooked and started knifing toward the little vessel as fast as he could. Without the cable on him, he became aware of a strange sensation. The waves were going one way, but the current was going the other. The current was so strong, the moving water propelled the swimmer right over the wave tops.

Haba arrived at the vessel in just a few seconds. Using a couple handles by the doorway, he pulled the top half of his body into the raft. Panting and out of breath, he focused on the faces inside. A bunch of wide-eyed people looked back at him.

"How's everyone doing?" asked the swimmer.

Silence.

"Are there any injuries?"

The survivors just stared at him.

Haba tried a new approach. "Does anyone have trouble swimming?"

A man who was hunched over in the center of the raft struggled to sit up and looked at Haba. It was Doug Faunt.

Haba looked back at him and asked, "Are you ready to go?"

"Yes, I'm ready," said Faunt.

"Okay, relax, and I'll take care of the rest."

Haba backed out of the cavelike shelter of the raft and into the howling wind and crashing seas. He waited at the doorway.

Faunt, weighed down by his water-filled survival suit, inched to the door. When he got his first leg out of the raft, the water drained into the foot area, swelling it to three times its normal size. He flopped into the water and floated on his back.

Haba wrapped his right arm around Faunt's chest. He started paddling with his other arm, using his flippers to thrust himself away from the raft. The swimmer kept glancing from the aircraft to the surrounding seas and back again, trying hard not to get blindsided by any big waves.

One big wave came thundering in on the men, but Haba saw it coming. He decided it was best to swim through it, rather than risk having it break directly on the survivor.

Up in the helicopter, Michael Lufkin began lowering the basket, watching in alarm as the wind sent it shooting fifty feet behind the aircraft. He brought the basket back inside. *Need to add weights to it,* he thought. Once that was done, he conned the pilots forward. Lufkin decided it best to let the basket hit the water in a spot where the waves would carry it to the swimmer.

"Okay, basket is in the water," he said over the headset. Then he did a double take while looking at the basket. Instead of being pushed by the waves, the basket drifted into and over the waves, away from Haba. And to make matters worse, the weights he just added made the basket sink rather than ride on the surface.

"Current took the basket, and the weights aren't working," said Lufkin. "I'm going to bring it back up and remove the weights."

Once that was done, he conned the pilots to a new hovering spot and let the basket hit the water just a few feet from Haba.

Despite the close proximity of the basket, the swimmer had to drag the survivor through two large waves to avoid their cascading white water. Faunt swallowed a considerable amount of seawater before Haba stuffed him into basket.

When Faunt was hauled into the aircraft and flopped out of the basket, he broke out into a wide grin.

"At that moment, I saw John Svendsen," recalled Faunt.

"I shouted his name, telling him I sure was glad to see him. I had been worrying about John and Dan, knowing how dedicated they were to the ship, the crew, and their responsibilities. I was afraid they would get caught up in their duties, and not get away from the capsized *Bounty* fast enough."

From below, Haba watched Faunt being hoisted. He figured he would try to save time by swimming back to the raft, which had now drifted almost two hundred yards away. He was swimming directly into most waves, being helped by the current. Sometimes a long wave, a comber, would slam him from the ten o'clock position and other times from the two o'clock side, driving him underwater. His progress seemed to take forever, and he realized he'd have nothing left in his tank if he continued this battle. Haba looked up at the helo and gave the signal to be picked up.

Once back inside the helicopter, he cupped his hands by Lufkin's ear. He shouted that there were still six people left in the raft and that no one appeared badly injured. "After we get the next survivor in the aircraft, just air-taxi me back to the raft! The current is unbelievable!"

"I know," said Lufkin. "It carried the basket the opposite way of the waves!"

The idea for an air-taxi—where Haba would be carried

just above the tops of the waves rather than lifted into the helicopter—would save precious seconds.

Pena updated Lufkin and Cerveny, telling them they had only twenty minutes to bingo time.

Once the pilots had repositioned the helicopter, Haba was lowered into the water, unhooked, swam to the raft, and stuck his head inside.

"Who's next?"

The survivors stayed quiet.

Haba looked at one of the female survivors closest to him and said, "Are you ready?" Jessica Black answered in the affirmative and off they went. This time the basket hoist went smoothly.

Haba used the next couple minutes to catch his breath, and soon the bare hook came down. He clipped the hook onto his harness. Just as he was about to give the thumbs-up signal to be lifted, he heard a roar, and out of the corner of his eye, he saw the monstrous sea bearing down on him. All he could do was hold his breath before being engulfed in a torrent of white water. The force of the wave was so strong, it ripped the mask and snorkel right off Haba's head.

Lufkin retracted cable as fast as he could and lifted

Haba out of the swirling foam before the next wave buried him.

Well, that was some wake-up call, thought Haba. *Just got to do the rescue with no mask.*

But the ocean wasn't quite done with him yet. When he arrived back at the raft and told the next survivor, Anna Sprague, to come out the doorway, a wave broke directly on the raft's canopy. Haba was hurled backward, landing ten feet from the raft. He coughed up a bellyful of water and kicked back to the raft, thinking, *This is not good. We gotta hurry, or we'll never get all these people out before bingo.*

In the cockpit, Cerveny was thinking the same thing. He knew another helo was on its way. He made up his mind—he wasn't going to put the survivors or his crew in danger by extending the bingo time. He also surmised that the survivors were in pretty good shape, because each time a new person came into the aircraft, the other survivors let out a cheer. *Just stay focused*, Cerveny told himself. *We're not done yet.*

In fact, he was so focused, he never saw the second helicopter speed by. But Pena did, and over the headset, she confirmed to both her crew and the C-130 that she had a visual on the other helicopter.

After Anna Sprague was safely in the helicopter, Haba extracted Warner without incident. *Now we're going good*, thought Haba. He treaded water, catching his breath, waiting to be air-taxied back to the life raft and the final three survivors.

At that same moment, Pena said, "Okay, we are at bingo."

"Roger," said Cerveny. "Lufkin, we're at bingo. After we get the swimmer up, we're going home."

Of course Haba didn't know this, and when he clipped onto the hook he was expecting to be brought back to the raft. Instead he found himself being lifted directly up, and he guessed that they were up against their fuel limit.

Once Haba was inside the helicopter, Lufkin hollered "RTB," which meant return to base.

"We still got three people down there!" shouted Haba.

"It's okay. There is another helo on scene and a third one coming. We hit bingo."

Lufkin grabbed the door handle and slid the door shut.

The five survivors, who had been hugging and crying tears of joy, all suddenly stopped. They stared at Lufkin, not understanding why they were leaving their friends below.

Haba, who also served as the aircraft's emergency medical technician, started going from survivor to survivor, telling them another aircraft would get their friends.

He also asked each survivor how they were feeling. Only Svendsen was seriously injured, and he was still vomiting from spending so much time being pounded by waves.

"Door is shut, and everyone is seated and ready to fly," said Lufkin over the headset.

"Roger," said Cerveny. Then he turned to Pena and said, "Take us home. You three did a heck of a job."

◄■■■►

Josh Scornavacchi, Matt Sanders, and John Jones spread out as best they could to keep the raft from flipping. The loud roar from the helicopter's rotors above them grew faint, and then the only sound was the surging seas. *They're probably just repositioning*, thought Scornavacchi.

The three men sat patiently, expecting to hear the welcoming *thwack-thwack-thwack* of the helicopter's return at any moment.

Scornavacchi peeked out the doorway, craning his neck so he could look up toward the sky. Rain and foam whipped at his exposed facial skin, and he was forced to retreat back inside the raft. Then he thought, *What if something happened to them?* He quickly changed his thinking. *Well, they know the three of us are in here. We just got to keep this raft afloat a little longer . . .*

CHAPTER 22

Catapulted

The second helicopter that reached the emergency scene had an extremely difficult job in front of them. Luckily, three of the four aircrew members in the second helo were quite experienced. In fact, aircraft commander Steve Bonn, age forty-four, was the pilot who had helped rescue Steve Cerveny when his helicopter crashed in the Rocky Mountains. Bonn had flown Blackhawk helicopters in the army for nine years and then joined the coast guard in 2000.

Flying with Bonn to the *Bounty* was flight mechanic, Gregory "Neil" Moulder, rescue swimmer Dan Todd, and copilot Jenny Fields. Moulder had more than fourteen years' experience hoisting rescue swimmers and survivors, and Todd had been a rescue swimmer for five years. Fields, a graduate of the Coast Guard Academy, was the newest of the crew, having been qualified to fly Jayhawks a year earlier.

All four had been called at home by Todd Farrell at the Operations Desk. He'd told them to report to the Air Station for a flight to a tall-ship sailing vessel taking on water. Dan Todd recalls getting the phone and asking, "What's a tall ship?"

"It looks like pirate ship," responded Farrell.

"This better not be a bad joke."

"No joke. It's real, all right, and you gotta come in right away."

Jenny Fields got the same call, but then her phone rang again. "I got a second phone call," recalls Fields, "just as I was leaving my driveway. It was Todd Farrell, and he told me that he needed me at the station *immediately*, that the sailors were abandoning ship that very moment. That's when my heart rate and adrenaline began pumping."

On the flight out, Steve Bonn said, "So who here has been to AHRS?" (Bonn was referring to Advanced Helicopter Rescue School, where crews practice in the towering surf at the Columbia Bar in Oregon.) Both Todd and

Moulder had gone through the training, and only Fields had not. Bonn gave her a quick overview of the additional duties of a copilot during extreme conditions.

"Watch the waves," said Bonn, who was sitting in the right seat, "and learn their timings, and give advisories as best you can. Be a vigilant safety pilot on the controls and instruments, but more specifically, be watching outside. I'm going to be mostly looking down and to the right during the hoists, so I need you to be looking everywhere else, and paint us a picture of what's out there."

Then the four-person crew discussed what they would do when they located survivors. All agreed that the swimmer would be put down in a sling deployment, followed by basket recoveries.

Todd got the usual butterflies in his stomach thinking through the steps he would take when he got into water. A mix of excitement and adrenaline was kicking in. He remembered how Randy Haba once told him, "Big cases don't come along very often, and for some of us, it's a once-in-a-lifetime experience. Everything you ever learned and practiced in training is going to be called upon."

When the crew arrived on the emergency scene, they had enough light to see without using their night-vision goggles, but depth perception was difficult. The only colors were shades of gray and white; gray water with white caps and variations of gray clouds all blurred by driving, horizontal rain. Wind tore the tops off the waves sending bits of white foam and spray, like giant snowflakes, up and into the air.

Peyton Russell, on the orbiting C-130, directed the helicopter toward the second *Bounty* life raft.

Bonn, who had the controls, edged the helicopter ever closer to the top of the waves. Suddenly, they could see the orange canopy of the life raft bouncing up and down in the seas like a cork in a raging river. Then a big wave rolled toward it and the raft disappeared behind the wall of water.

The commander felt a building tension as he slowed the helicopter and got ready for the hoists—if there were hoists. No one knew for sure if the second *Bounty* life raft had survivors in it. Bonn, however, was certain of one thing: If the sailors were not in the life raft, he would have to spend precious time and fuel investigating promising strobe lights. Fields had calculated bingo at 2,200 pounds of fuel to return to Elizabeth City. She also calculated lesser amounts if they went to Marine Station Cherry Point, or had to set down on the nearest point of land, which was the beach at Cape Hatteras.

Looking down through the windshield of the aircraft, Fields could clearly see the raft in the crashing chaos of foam and water. *Come on, come on, someone show yourself. There's got to be people in there*, she thought.

Fields focused on two access door flaps, but no heads stuck out. The helicopter was now just fifty feet above the raft and was buffeted by strong crosswinds. *Where are they?* Suddenly, she saw the canopy door open and three faces in red Gumby suits looked directly up at her. *Yes!* Then the survivors started waving their arms. Fields could almost feel their relief, knowing they were not alone.

Bonn positioned the aircraft in a hover, nose into the wind. They were about twenty-five feet above the tallest wave tops. Fields set the radar altimeter at twenty feet: If a wave came closer than twenty feet to the aircraft, an audible advisory would warn them that they were dangerously close to the crest.

After the team went through the final check list, Todd positioned himself at the door and Moulder lowered him toward the water. As soon as the swimmer's flippers touched the ocean, he straightened his arms and plunged out of the sling. It was a fifty-yard sprint to the raft, and Todd felt he had never swum so fast in his life. All that pent-up adrenaline could finally be used.

At the raft, Todd pulled himself completely inside the doorway. He sat down and faced the survivors, then yanked out his snorkel and raised his mask. After taking a couple deep breaths, he said, "Hey, I'm Dan. I hear you guys need a ride."

Unlike the first raft, this group of survivors was animated, with a couple yelling, "Way to go! You guys are awesome!"

Todd was hoping his casual greeting would give the survivors a feeling of confidence, as if swimming through thirty-foot breaking seas in a hurricane was an everyday occurrence for him.

"How many people in here?" asked Todd.

"Six."

"Nobody has fallen out?"

"No."

Todd pulled a small waterproof radio transmitter from his vest, turned it on, and made contact with Fields. "There are six people in the raft." Then he put the radio away and turned back to the survivors, asking, "Does anyone have any injuries?"

The survivors pointed to Prokosh.

"Okay, he will go first. This is how I need you all to do this for me. When I get you to the basket, you're to sit inside and keep your hands and feet inside. The quicker you do that, the quicker you will get into the helicopter."

Just then, a giant wave slammed into the raft, first hitting the spot where Todd was perched, catapulting him into the air. He flew toward the other side of the raft, accidently clotheslining two people on the way, and landed in a heap on a survivor. Water roared in after him, as if someone with a firehouse was aiming it through the doorway.

"Is anyone hurt?" shouted Todd, crawling back toward the door.

"We're okay!"

Todd wasted no time exiting the raft—he couldn't risk having another wave hit the raft and injure him. If that happened, the survivors would be at the mercy of the seas until the next helicopter arrived.

Todd wanted to get Prokosh out of the raft and into the basket immediately. He was trained to always take the injured survivor first, when the rescue swimmer had maximum energy. Should the survivor be torn from his grip by a wave, Todd would want to be able to get that person fast because they may not be able to stay afloat for long.

He looked at Prokosh and shouted, "Can you get out of the raft?"

"I'll do whatever it takes," said Prokosh. "I got in the raft somehow and I can get out."

Todd motioned for him to exit the raft. Prokosh clawed his way to the door. He stuck his head out and then struggled to lift one leg higher than the tubing that encircled the raft and eventually got that leg into the ocean. Then with a push he dropped into the water and rolled onto his back.

Todd wrapped his right arm around Prokosh's chest, and began putting distance between them and the raft. With such high winds, the swimmer wanted to get the survivor at least forty feet from the raft so that the helicopter could stay downwind of it. If the aircraft was over the raft, its rotor wash might flip it.

Steve Bonn had a bird's-eye view of the raft at the two o'clock position. He knew that the wind and current would make the hoists more difficult than anything they'd experienced. The commander watched Todd and the survivor taken by the current and pushed upwind from the raft. Bonn would have to move in that direction, passing directly over the raft. Without any other choice, he moved the aircraft forward so he could keep the swimmer in view, and he held his breath.

Thankfully, the raft stayed upright.

Bonn awaited conning from Moulder. It was impossible to hold the aircraft in one position with wind gusts sending it lurching forward, backward, or side to side. Despite Bonn's best efforts, any movement on the control levers, no matter how subtle, would send the aircraft rocketing ten feet or more.

"Big wave coming from the left," said Fields in as calm a voice as possible.

Bonn increased altitude another ten feet, letting the wave slide beneath them. Then he descended again, knowing the closer he was to the water, the easier the hoist would be for Moulder.

Moulder had the basket ready at the doorway and shoved it out. He started letting cable out. When the basket was halfway down, a crosswind caught it, shooting it forward and to the right. Moulder was on his stomach now, trying to steady the cable, telling the pilots what was happening. He glanced ahead to where Todd held the survivor and couldn't believe how quickly the current was moving them.

Just as Moulder was about to con Bonn to a new position, the wind changed and blew the basket backward and left. Moulder let out cable as fast as he could and saw the basket hit the water.

"Hold right there! Hold!" barked Moulder over the headset. The basket was only a few feet from the swimmer and survivor, and he could see they would reach it without too much trouble.

On the headset, Moulder could hear the automated voice coming from the radar altimeter saying, "Altitude! Altitude!" He knew a particularly large wave had come within their comfort zone. He tried to ignore the warning—that was the pilot's worry. He had to keep his eye on the basket and survivor.

Moulder watched as the survivor was put in the basket. Todd gave the thumbs-up signal, and Moulder started retracting cable as fast as he could. The basket, heavy with the survivor's weight, swung like a pendulum. Moulder, now on his knees, struggled to stabilize it.

"Basket is coming up," said Moulder. Then five seconds later, out of breath, he gasped, "Basket at the door." Then grunting, "Bringing basket inside the cabin."

Moulder used all his strength to lift the survivor—including the fifty extra pounds of water in the survival suit—into the cabin.

"Couple really big ones coming . . . ," Fields said, referring to the waves.

Bonn dared to take his eyes off the swimmer drifting up and over the waves, and saw two mountains of water approaching, their crests a snarling mess of white water.

CHAPTER 23

Flipped Like a Pancake

MONDAY, APPROXIMATELY 8:00 A.M. TO 9:30 A.M., OCTOBER 30

While Bonn powered the helicopter up and out of reach of the big waves, Todd, down in the ocean, wasn't so lucky. He saw the first comber out of the corner of his eye and managed to take a big breath and dive downward into it, the same as a person might do at the seashore when they fear a breaking wave is going to knock them over.

Holding his breath, Todd could feel himself get tumbled. But he knew he was much safer under the water than in the maw of the wave on the surface. He let the moving mountain slide pass, then fought to the surface.

Blowing water out of his snorkel, he was preparing to take in a deep lungful of air when the second wave caught him, driving him deep. Todd's entire body screamed for oxygen. He kicked and stroked toward the light, toward the surface. When his head popped out of the foam, he coughed up green water, trying to clear his lungs.

Fortunately, the next wave was a small swell, and he let the current push him up and over it. He was far from the raft, and didn't even think about swimming to it. Instead, he treaded water, waiting for Moulder to get the survivor out of the basket and lower the hook.

In the cabin, Prokosh struggled to get out of the basket. First, he pivoted so he could be on his knees, then lifted his chest out while placing his hands on the helicopter floor. Some water sloshed out of the neck of the survival suit, but most slid downward, collecting at his feet, making it look like he had enormous clown shoes on.

Moulder grabbed Prokosh under the arms and helped get his legs out of the basket. Then he motioned for Prokosh to crawl toward the front of the aircraft to allow more room for removing the basket. Moulder worked as fast as he could, but a nagging voice inside his head was saying to speed things up. He tried to balance haste with precision—one mistake could put the whole rescue in jeopardy. For a moment, he considered asking how much time to bingo, but pushed the notion aside. *Just focus on what I can control*, he told himself.

Steve Bonn kept watch on Todd and updated Moulder. "I've got eyes on the swimmer. He is being pulled far from the raft, so we're going to have to pick him up. No way he will be able to swim back."

"Roger," said Moulder. "Stand by. I'm disconnecting the basket now."

A minute later, Moulder lowered the hook to Todd, who clipped it to his harness. By prearrangement, Todd was hoisted just above the wave tops and air-taxied toward the raft.

Moulder later recalled a frightening moment when he was looking down at Todd: "He was swinging like a wrecking ball because his fins were acting like sails. I grabbed hold of the swaying cable to steady it, and that's when I felt my shoulder pop."

Moulder had dislocated his shoulder but, there was nothing he could do about it at that moment, because the raft had just come into view. "Okay, ah . . . forward and right fifteen feet," he panted.

Todd was carried to within twenty feet of the raft. Moulder put him in the water, watched him unclip, and started retracting the cable. The pain in his shoulder was radiating outward into his arm and down his back. He thought, *We can't abort this mission because of me.*

Moulder decided he'd fix the problem himself. Positioning himself sideways to his jump seat, he took a deep breath and then launched himself—injured shoulder first—into the seat. A searing, burning sensation shot through his arm, but he felt the shoulder go back in the socket.

Adam Prokosh—in his own painful state from the fractured discs—watched him with wide eyes, not sure why the hoist operator threw himself into the seat. He wanted to ask what happened, but the rotors were too loud, and the hoist operator was already racing to reattach the basket.

Rescue swimmer Dan Todd had a more difficult challenge reaching the raft than he did the first time. He was in the midst of a series of waves that seemed ever more chaotic. "One minute," he later explained, "a big wave approached from the back and I'd be body surfing, but then the surge of the wave would carry my legs right over the top of my head and I'd have to ball up a little to avoid getting my back broken."

The waves were going toward the raft, but the current was moving the opposite way. Although Todd repeated the process of body surfing, balling up, then swimming, he still couldn't get to the raft. "Just when I'd get the hang of these waves coming up from behind me, another wave would materialize off to my side. It would slap me in the face, rolling me sideways. They were absolutely crazy. But it was the current that really made everything so difficult."

It became a frustrating journey, trying to cover a mere twenty feet in such a strong current. He'd body-surf a wave tantalizingly close to the raft, but as the wave passed Todd, it collided with the raft, pushing the vessel beyond reach.

Todd's arm hit something in the foam and he grabbed it with his hand. A fifty-foot half-inch line trailed from the raft. Attached to it was a parachute-shaped "sea anchor" made of fabric, intended to slow and stabilize the raft. The rescue swimmer held on tight, and let a wave push him forward. Then he pulled in a couple feet of slack until the wave hit the raft and straightened out the line, pulling Todd along, about three feet below the surface. The next wave propelled the swimmer forward, and again he hauled in a couple more feet of slack before being towed behind the raft.

"I couldn't help but notice that while being dragged,"

Todd remembered, "how peaceful it seemed just a few feet below the surface. It was actually quite beautiful, and if I looked downward, the visibility was excellent. Then when I'd come to the surface, it was complete chaos, like being inside a washing machine. The difference was so unexpected, it was striking."

After three or four of these rides, Todd reached the raft, and motioned for the next survivor to come out. This hoist went like clockwork. The basket was just a few feet away, partly because Moulder was learning to gage the waves and current, but also because Steve Bonn had maneuvered the aircraft to a mere ten feet above the wave tops.

Normally, the helo would be a good thirty feet above the biggest waves, but Bonn knew the lower he positioned the aircraft the less time the basket would be in the air and blown around. Bonn relied on Fields to warn him when a big wave was coming. He ignored the continuous cautionary voice from the radar altimeter squawking, "Altitude, altitude."

Fields was juggling her duties. One minute she was monitoring the instruments, and then she'd manage the communications with the orbiting C-130. She also had to recalculate the fuel burn and operate the in-flight camera.

She was looking through the camera to find Todd in the whitewash below when she reminded herself to scan the seas again. Just as her head was turning to look out the side window, something caught her eye in the chin bubble window down by her feet. A snarling peak at the top of a giant wave was rushing up toward the belly of the helicopter.

Bonn felt the pressure on his collective (the control lever for altitude) as Fields took over the collective and announced in a hurried voice, "Up! Up! Up!" Together the two pilots sent the helo climbing, barely escaping the extreme wave.

Todd, treading water, watched the helo shoot upward. He was relieved to see they dodged the two-story wave and got the survivor safely in the aircraft. Just as he pivoted to see if the raft was close enough to try to swim to, he witnessed every rescue swimmer's nightmare. A big wave caught the raft just right and lifted it almost completely out of the water, flipping it like a pancake. Now the raft's black bottom was on the surface. The orange canopy was completely submerged.

A sense of panic shot through Todd. *Where are the people?* He started swimming with every ounce of strength he had.

Fields saw the whole thing happen in slow motion. "I'd been scanning in all directions for extreme waves. I was thinking that even though the magnitude of the seas was bigger than anything I'd seen, what really got my attention was the speed they were going. A mass of water moving that fast possesses an extraordinary amount of raw energy. I marveled that Dan was in the midst of them. Then I looked toward the raft just in time to see it flip. Both Steve and I gasped, then watched Dan sprinting toward it."

The raft likely flipped because with two fewer survivors in it, the vessel was both lighter and perhaps unbalanced. Strong rotor wash from the aircraft might also have assisted the wave in launching the raft into the air.

The fear that people were either drowning or fighting to get out of the upside down raft gave Todd an extra boost of strength. He swam and body-surfed quickly toward the raft, prepared to either dive down and through the doorway or perhaps cut through the fabric floor if he had to.

Just as he arrived, heads started popping up, and he counted all four remaining people hanging onto the outer lifeline encircling the raft.

"Are you okay?" shouted Todd to the group.

Someone yelled back, "We're good."

Todd made a split decision not to try to right the capsized raft. *The raft is enormous,* he thought. *It may take forever to get it right-side up. They have something to hold on to, and they all have survival suits and floatation vests. Let's get them out of here.*

"Okay," Todd hollered, looking at the person closest to him, "you're next. Just relax and follow my directions."

The decision not to re-right the raft was the correct one, and it had the added benefit of making the remaining rescues go quicker. The survivors were already outside the vessel and ready to go. Over the next twenty minutes, all four sailors were successfully hoisted up.

Moulder was exhausted from nonstop hoisting and wrestling the loaded basket into the cabin over and over. But when he was finished with the sailors and was looking down at Todd, he had a chance to smile. He saw Todd pull out his knife and stab the raft. Procedure called for sinking empty life rafts so no other aircrafts or vessels would get in a dangerous position by trying a rescue that wasn't needed. But what made Moulder grin was that the raft had several compartments, and Todd had to repeatedly stab the raft to get it to start sinking.

"At first," recalled Moulder, "I wondered what he was doing . . . It looked like he was trying to kill some creature from a horror movie, and the creature was winning."

Fields glanced behind her in the cabin where the survivors were packed like sardines. Most were quiet, still in a daze or in outright shock from their ordeal. Fields radioed the C-130 that they now had all six survivors safely in the cabin and that they were about to pick up their swimmer. Peyton Russell suggested that when they got the rescue swimmer safely onboard that they investigate a possible PIW (person in water) before they moved on to the other *Bounty* life raft with the remaining three survivors.

About this time, Todd was lifted into the helicopter. He slumped against a survivor, panting and trying to get his breath, after thirty-five minutes of nonstop exertion. He thought how in rescue-swimmer school he went through the "six-man multi," in which trainees had to rescue six "drowning" instructors in half an hour. And he remembered that the rescue-swimmer manual required swimmers to have the strength to perform in heavy seas for thirty minutes. *Well, that's what I did. I guess I earned my pay getting these six people.*

A wave of nausea rolled over Todd, partly because he had swallowed so much seawater, and partly because he was coming down off the adrenaline buzz and his body was crashing. He wondered how long it would take to get back to base.

Just then Moulder leaned in close to Todd and said, "The other helicopter had to leave because of fuel. But there are still three people in the raft. Mr. Bonn wants to know if you feel strong enough to get back in the water . . ."

CHAPTER 24

Running Out of Time

If the helo has enough gas to keep going, I'm going to keep going, too, thought Todd. He shouted to Moulder, "Tell Mr. Bonn yes."

Fields later recalled how they first took a few moments to investigate the possible PIW. "We came across some debris, mostly survival gear out of the overturned life rafts, along with a couple empty Gumby suits. After a quick search, we had to get to the raft with the three remaining people in it because we were getting low on fuel."

Bonn put the Jayhawk in a hover near the raft, and down went Todd, now swimming markedly slower than earlier. To save time, he did not enter the raft. He knew that rescue swimmer Randy Haba had already briefed the sailors earlier when he extracted four of the seven. Todd also remembered how when he was inside the first raft he was thrown from one side to the other, nearly injuring some of the survivors. He wanted to avoid that possibility. So instead he stuck his head inside the vessel and hollered, "It's only three of you, right?"

The survivors acknowledged in the affirmative. Todd then asked about injuries, and they said they had none. "Okay!" shouted Todd, "we gotta move fast." Then he pointed to the person closest to him and hollered, "You first!"

He put the survivor in the basket without incident, and when he looked back at the raft, he saw that it had flipped. *Not again!*

Just as before, Todd put his head down and began sprinting to the overturned raft. Only this time, his depleted energy was no match for the waves and current. *I'll never make it.* Both his arms and legs felt as heavy as tree trunks. Instead of stroking and kicking smartly through water, the sensation was as if trying to push through mud. Rolling over on his back, he looked up at the aircraft and saw Moulder crouched by the open cabin door. Todd gave the thumbs-up signal, meaning he needed to be picked up. He prayed that the last two people in the raft had escaped and were holding onto the lifeline.

Rather than go into the helicopter, Todd was hoisted above the wave tops and air-taxied toward the raft. He looked down, and was startled to see the raft's orange canopy. Somehow the survivors had righted the raft, or perhaps a wave had flipped it back over. Todd could only hope the survivors were inside.

Once in the water, Todd felt a surge of relief: Two heads poked out of the raft's doorway. The rescue swimmer fought his way closer. Without any coaxing, one of the survivors slid into the water. Todd started towing him away from the raft to await the lowering of the basket. The two men were slammed by a wave, and Todd ingested a considerable amount of seawater during their tumble. When he popped to the surface, he still had the survivor in his grip. Todd vomited repeatedly, willing himself to hang on to the survivor as the seas tried to tug him away.

Fields had watched Todd put the first of the last two survivors in the basket. When the survivor entered the helicopter, she thought, *Why are they so slow? Don't they know we're running out of time?*

The copilot didn't know it, but this survivor had one of his arms outside the basket as it approached the doorway. Moulder had to lean out and smack the person's arm back inside. (An arm or even a hand outside the basket could be broken in multiple places if it gets trapped between the aircraft and steel basket.) The survivor may have been reluctant about leaving the basket once in the aircraft after the slap. Moulder didn't waste time. He yanked him out, unclipped the basket and put the hook down for Todd, who had drifted far from the raft.

Todd clipped the cable to his harness once it arrived. As he was being lifted from a trough, he swung forward ten feet, directly into the face of a big sea wave coming from a different angle than the others. He slammed into the liquid wall, and spray from the impact shot high in the sky before the swimmer emerged on the other side of the wave.

Bonn, worried about both fuel and the swimmer, said, "I hope I'm not swinging him too much. Just hold him below the aircraft and we will reposition him by the raft."

"Roger," answered Moulder, "I'm going to bring him halfway up."

Todd careened wildly below the aircraft, and Moulder, hanging on to the cable with his left arm, almost got yanked out the door.

Once the helicopter was near the raft, Moulder set Todd down into the water. He watched Todd unclip and begin methodically stroking. The flight mechanic wondered just how much strength Todd had left: *You can do it. Just one more left.*

Bonn was thinking the same thing. As if to will his swimmer more power, he blurted out, "Come on, Todd, reach that raft!"

An agonizingly slow minute went by, where it looked like the current was getting the best of their swimmer. Then Bonn spoke again, this time with a sense of relief. "Todd has the towline!"

The swimmer pulled himself to the raft and helped the last survivor out. As Todd was getting the final sailor inside the basket, the two were pushed by a wave from the right to the left side of the helicopter.

Moulder's heart skipped a beat. He craned his neck out the door to search underneath the helo for the two men. As soon as he saw that the survivor was in the basket, he retracted the cable as fast as he could.

"This one is swinging really bad," said Moulder.

Bonn didn't respond, but instead kept his focus on holding the helicopter as still as possible. He felt the seconds tick by. *We've got to get this guy in and then get the*

swimmer in, within five minutes or we're going to be up
against our bingo.

Fields felt the same tension. When the survivor was at the door, she looked over her shoulder and saw Moulder yank him in. "When the last survivor was pulled inside," she later recalled, "I got really mad. Instead of getting out of the basket immediately, he put his hands up and cheered. I remember wanting to hit him upside the head and shout GET OUT OF THE BASKET! I know they had just been in the worst situation of their lives, and I should have been more forgiving, but getting Dan back in the helo and getting home safely depended on our fuel, and time is fuel."

With the last *Bounty* sailor out of the raft, the exhausted rescue swimmer slashed the raft with his knife and was lifted back to the helicopter. After he regained his breath, Todd and Moulder grilled the survivors about the exact number of people on the ship. Earlier reports had said sixteen or seventeen, and they were able to confirm the correct number was sixteen. The first helicopter had extracted five, and this helo had nine jammed in the cabin, so two were still missing. By process of elimination the group now knew that everyone was accounted for except Christian, Captain Walbridge, and First Mate Svendsen. The crew also knew that the first helicopter had plucked one single sailor drifting alone out of the sea—they just didn't know that person was John Svendsen, so they feared for him as well.

Commander Bonn and Fields knew they were almost at bingo, but because they always planned for a small cushion of fuel, they decided to do one last loop around the search area, hoping to spot a survivor. All they found was more debris. Bonn made sure the crew went through its final checklist to ensure everything not needed was turned off. Then he punched in the coordinates for Elizabeth City, and turned over the controls to Fields.

While Fields was flying the helo, Bonn used the aircraft's computer to predict fuel burn rate for landing at Elizabeth City. He updated the systems with the current headwinds, and the system flashed "bingo fuel," meaning they would not be landing with as much of a cushion as they thought. In fact, should the headwinds increase, they might be in an emergency situation of their own.

Fields's heart sank and her stomach felt like there was "a boulder in it." *What have I done?* she thought. *I failed everyone. This is my fault if the headwinds are worse than expected and we have to ditch.*

Bonn read her mind and tried to reassure her. Still, both pilots knew they'd be cutting it close and would have to fly in an exact straight line; they could not let the winds push them even a few feet off course.

As the pilots discussed fuel and contingency landing plans, the survivors settled in for what was anticipated to be a two-hour, turbulent-filled flight back to land. One by one the sailors began to fall asleep.

One survivor couldn't get the image of Christian, Walbridge, and Svendsen out of his thoughts. Two of those three people were at the mercy of the seas. The survivor crawled closer to Moulder and asked, "Are there any ships going for the last two people? We can't just leave them out there. I don't even want to think about the possibility that they didn't make it."

Moulder tried to console the man. "We are very good at what we do. We will find your friends. A third helicopter is coming out."

On that third helicopter, flown by pilots Brian Bailey and Nick Hazlett, flight mechanic Tim Kuklewski was awestruck by the sight of *Bounty*. "When we arrived at the *Bounty*," he recalled, "I was surprised by how big it was. I took my iPhone out, aimed it out the doorway, and snapped off three quick shots."

Kuklewski and his crewmates saw how the debris field stretched for miles. With the C-130 guiding them, they hovered as low as possible over promising survival suits. Some suits were quickly identified as empty because they were folded over or were clearly flat, but others were filled with a combination of air and water, making it look like a person was inside. For these suits, pilots Bailey and Hazlett kept approaching them from all different angles.

"Rescue swimmer Tim Bolen and I kept getting our hopes up," said Kuklewski. "We were hoping to see a face or maybe a hand rise out of the water. We would not fly off until we were one hundred percent sure they were empty." But time and time again, the suits were unmanned, and after more than an hour of searching, they too hit their bingo. The flight team headed back to Elizabeth City, where they rested and refueled, preparing to head back out later that day.

A fourth helicopter was launched at noon, and they resumed the search. Rather than go to *Bounty*, which had been examined several times, this crew followed the debris field a full two miles out from the ship. The crew consisted of pilots Matt Herring and Kristen Jaekel, flight mechanic Ryan Parker, and swimmer Casey Hanchette.

They scanned the storm-tossed seas below them, hoping for some sign of life. After completing the first search pattern and coming up empty, they began their second search. Parker noticed how one Gumby suit floated differently from the others. "It was more spread out than the others suits we investigated, so we came back around and got in a low hover. Then the hood of the suit flopped open and we could see blond hair."

Rescue swimmer Hanchette was immediately lowered. In the water, he unhooked and swam toward the unconscious sailor, who was floating facedown. The sailor was Claudene Christian. Hanchette immediately got her in the sling and clipped his harness back on the hook, and they were lifted up to the helicopter together. He and Parker administered CPR the entire hour and a half ride back to the air station. But their nonstop efforts were for naught: Christian was dead.

Christian had a laceration on her nose, but otherwise showed no other signs of trauma. We will never know if she survived for a time in the water or if she was pulled down by the rigging and died quickly. The sad fact was that after an incredible rescue of fourteen people by the coast guard, one *Bounty* crew member had been taken by the hurricane, and Captain Walbridge was still missing. The odds of him being found alive were shrinking with each passing hour.

CHAPTER 25

Held by the Sea

When the survivors touched down at Elizabeth City, they were swarmed by people trying to help: police, paramedics, coast guard, and Red Cross. Those sailors still in survival suits needed help exiting the helicopters because of all the water inside their suits. It quickly became apparent that they could barely take a step. Rescue swimmers and flight mechanics asked the survivors to sit on the edge of the helicopter doorway while slits were cut in the feet of the Gumby suits to let the water drain out.

Once off the aircraft and inside the station, coast guard officials interviewed everyone. At that particular time, Christian and Captain Walbridge had not been found. The search and rescue team was desperate to find out anything that would help in their efforts.

Adam Prokosh was treated at a hospital for his separated shoulder and the fractured vertebrae in his back. He was then reunited with the rest of the survivors at a hotel, where he shared a room with Josh Scornavacchi. A couple hours later, they learned that Christian had been found but was unresponsive. Some thought that meant that she was alive, but a short time later word came back that Christian had died.

"Right after we found out," said Scornavacchi, "the Red Cross came to the hotel, and we boarded cabs to go to Walmart to get some clothes. Everyone was crying because we had just learned Claudene didn't make it."

Christian's parents, Dina and Rex, had been worried about their daughter since *Bounty* first set sail from New London. Their anxiety had only increased when Christian called them at the beginning of the voyage to tell them how much she loved them. Their concern mounted even more when they later received the text message from Christian that said:

If I go down with the ship and the worst happens, just know that I AM TRULY, GENUINELY HAPPY. And I'm doing what I love! I love you.

Days of sickening worry passed and then came the dreaded phone call from the coast guard when Christian was first located and lifted into the helicopter. The Christians were told Claudene Christian was unresponsive and being given CPR. Dina and Rex immediately began flying on a series of connecting flights to get to Elizabeth City as fast as possible.

While waiting for one of the connecting flights in Atlanta, Dina's cell phone suddenly rang. It was a doctor at the hospital where Christian's body was taken, and he broke the news that she had died. The Christians were heartbroken, but also angry. *How could this have happened?* they wondered. *How could an experienced captain set sail when the whole world knew a hurricane was heading in their direction?*

And as images of the sinking *Bounty* glowed from television sets across the United States, the entire country was asking the same question. Part of that answer is held by the sea. After searching twelve thousand overlapping square nautical miles, the coast guard suspended the search for Captain Robin Walbridge. His body was never found.

THE END

GLOSSARY

AFT: At, in, close to, or toward the stern.

ALOFT: At or toward the upper rigging.

BACKSTAY: A rope or shroud extending from the top of the mast aft to the ship's side or stern to help support the mast.

BAROMETER: An instrument used to measure atmospheric pressure, which can help predict weather.

BEAM: The breadth of a ship at its widest point.

BILGE: The lowest inner part of a ship.

BINGO: A coast guard term that pilots use when they must head back to base because of low fuel.

BOSUN: A ship's deck officer.

BOW: The front section of a ship or boat.

CAULK: To make a boat watertight by packing the seams with string and tar.

FORECASTLE: The forward part of a ship usually below the exposed deck.

HEEL: The leaning of a ship to one side or another.

HELM: The steering mechanism of a ship; the wheel.

IMMERSION SUIT: A protective garment that offers warmth against cold water. Helps keep body heat trapped inside.

KEEL: The principle structural member of a ship, running fore and aft on the center line, extending from bow to stern, and forming the backbone of the vessel.

MATE: A high-ranking deck officer.

MIZZEN: A fore and aft sail set on a mast in the middle of the ship.

MUSTER: A gathering of a crew.

NIGHT-VISION GOGGLES: A device that allows the person wearing it to see objects on a dark night.

REEF: A portion of a sail rolled and tied down to lessen the area exposed to the wind.

RIGGING: The system of ropes, chains, and tackle used to support and control the masts, sails, and yards of a sailing vessel.

RUB RAIL: A horizontal piece of wood attached to the outermost portions of the hull used to protect the underlying timbers.

SPANKER: A four-sided sail set fore and aft on the rear mast.

SPAR: A wooden or metal pole used as a mast, yard, or any other way to support rigging.

STERN: The rear of the ship.

YARD: A long, tapering spar slung at right angles to the mast to support and spread a square sail.

AUTHORS' NOTES

Michael Tougias

When *Bounty* was first encountering heavy seas, I was, coincidentally, on TV talking about storms. One of the hosts asked me if I thought there might be any ships in harm's way with Sandy coming up the eastern seaboard. I paused and then explained that the storm had been so well forecasted that all ships would be in port. Imagine my surprise when, two days later, news reports of a dramatic rescue of *Bounty* splashed across my TV set. That launched my quest to learn more, and later I contacted Doug Campbell to team up and try to write the definitive account of what happened and why.

What struck me during my research was how much worse this accident could have been. The sailors donning of survival suits and gathering on deck literally occurred just minutes before the ship rolled to its side. Had they been below deck during the capsizing, I doubt anyone would have gotten out alive, especially because there was just a single passageway to the top.

Equally important was the coast guard's decision to

launch Wes McIntosh's C-130 into the heart of the storm. If that plane had not been on scene when *Bounty* heeled over, the loss of life would have been higher, because at that time the aircraft was the only communication link between the ship and the outside world. Without the C-130 crew to relay the disaster back to Elizabeth City, the helicopter commanded by Steve Cerveny would not have launched until at least two hours later. The immediate launch of that helo likely saved the life of John Svendsen who was floating alone in the raging sea, far from both *Bounty* and the life rafts.

The airlift rescue of the first five sailors is remarkable not only because it occurred in hurricane-force winds and thirty-foot seas, but it was also done in the dark. And the second helicopter had just as dangerous a task. They had to extract a total of nine sailors from two different rafts under tight time constraints due to fuel limitations.

President Obama had it right when he lauded the coast guard. Speaking in New Jersey just after the storm struck, he said, "One of my favorite stories is down in North Carolina where the coast guard was going out to save a sinking ship. They sent the rescue swimmer out and the rescue swimmer said, 'Hi, I'm Dan, I understand you guys need a ride.' That kind of spirit of resilience and strength—but most importantly looking out for one another—that's why we always bounce back from these kinds of disasters."

We often think of the coast guard as "just doing their jobs," because most are humble and downplay their role. We assume that when one mission is complete, they move right on to the next. And they do, but every now and then a rescue or rescue attempt comes along that moves the rescuers deeply and has an impact that will last well beyond their careers. I recall how Mike Myers, the copilot on the C-130 with Wes McIntosh, wrote to me saying, "It was so painful to experience the *Bounty* crew's emotional highs and lows. There was a bond and connection between our crew and theirs. Then to have them go in the water, at night, exhausted, and hastily forced overboard, it became our worst-case scenario. It was heartbreaking thinking that the worst had happened."

The survivors knew it was a combination of their own gritty determination to live coupled with the coast guard's resolve to find and rescue them that has allowed them to have more tomorrows. But for some, the ordeal wasn't over after the rescue and they were plagued with nightmares and post-traumatic stress, and they were subject to being second-guessed by others.

Not all of the survivors wanted to talk about their *Bounty* experience, and who could blame them? They endured a period of constant high-level stress, near drowning, the loss of friends they loved, and a barrage of media requests. They also had to relive what happened during their testimony at the Coast Guard Inquiry. It was held in front of a packed hearing room that included the owner of *Bounty*, the parents of Claudene Christian, and attorneys for the Christian family, who later filed a multimillion-dollar lawsuit against the Bounty Organization. It was not, nor has it been, an easy time for some of the crew.

━━━

Robin Walbridge's disastrous decision to leave port is the way most people will remember him. But we have all made mistakes, and it seems unfair that over a lifetime of difficult choices a person gets labeled for their last one. Coast Guard Captain Eric Jones explained it this way: "One bad decision does not undo all the positive influence Robin Walbridge had on sailors." I think he's right, and almost every crew member who survived Sandy agrees—they almost all spoke highly of Robin's leadership and training skills.

We also need to remember that Hurricane Sandy was unlike other hurricanes. It was epic—nine-hundred miles wide, the largest storm ever recorded in the North Atlantic. Captain Walbridge and all those who followed him as he steered *Bounty* out of New London, Connecticut, believed they could skirt the storm. And maybe if it was a "typical" hurricane, they might have done just that. But Sandy's reach was so massive that by the time they realized its magnitude, there was no safe direction to sail.

Still, the captain should have thought of his crew first and not that "a ship is safer at sea than at port" during a storm.

A critical decision point in this book occurs in the opening pages when Captain Walbridge calls the crew together to announce his plans to sail despite the oncoming storm. He told them anyone could leave and he wouldn't think any less of them or hold it against them. Why, I wondered, did every single crew member agree to remain on the ship? Most said they had confidence in the captain, the ship, and their own training. But I think there was another, more subtle factor at work—the group itself.

Perhaps no one wanted to be the first to walk off *Bounty*, appear to be afraid, or be perceived as letting their fellow crewmates down. Remember, most of the crew were under thirty years old, and they felt loyalty to one another and to the captain, without the benefit of decades of sailing. Also, the manner in which Captain Walbridge made this announcement likely influenced the outcome. The crew was forced to make a quick decision, without having the time to check various forecasts themselves. Nor did they have the luxury to sleep on their decision, discuss it with family, or have a private conversation with the captain. Instead, when no one spoke up and said they were leaving, the captain ordered them to prepare the ship for getting underway.

When I think of *Bounty*, a cascade of thoughts flows through me. I recall how I went on the ship briefly twenty years ago with my father and my son in Fall River, Massachusetts. I thought she was beautiful. When I was just fifteen years old, I consumed the trilogy of books related to the original *Bounty* written by Charles Nordhoff and James Norman Hall in the 1930s (*Mutiny on the Bounty, Men Against the Sea,* and *Pitcairn's Island.*) They were wonderful stories and likely fueled my future writing career and love of the sea. Now when I reflect on the *Bounty*, I feel mostly sadness. My thoughts are of that majestic old ship in its death throes and how Sandy took the lives of two crew members. But what bothers me most is that it didn't have to happen.

Douglas Campbell

Jan Miles, cocaptain of the tall ship *Pride of Baltimore II*, wrote a scalding "open letter" to Captain Robin Walbridge and posted it on the internet a month after *Bounty* sank. In that letter, Miles echoed the sentiments of many in the maritime community when he asked:

"Why did you throw all caution away by navigating for a close pass of Hurricane Sandy? I was so surprised to discover that *Bounty* was at sea near Cape Hatteras and close to Hurricane Sandy Sunday night October 28th! That decision of yours was reckless in the extreme!"

There were few among the dozens of individuals—other than *Bounty* crew members—interviewed by Mike Tougias and I who disagreed with Miles. One who did was Cliff Bredeson, an occasional volunteer *Bounty* crew member who had made numerous ocean crossings with Walbridge.

Bredeson said that in his opinion, Walbridge's decision to leave New London was appropriate. Had the pumps not failed, *Bounty* would have been fine, Bredeson told me.

I am a sailor of small boats and have logged numerous miles offshore—far, far fewer than Robin Walbridge. In that limited experience, I have made my share of decisions to sail that I've later regretted. I've been lucky. While some of those decisions have led to discomfort, none has led to disaster.

When I heard *Bounty*'s story in October 2012, I—like most other sailors—wondered why a captain would think his crew would be safer at sea in a hurricane than on shore. To be absolutely clear, the safest way to deal with boats is to stay off them. There always are risks involved with going to sea, some of which cannot be anticipated. But the ocean floor is littered with the wreckage of ships— particularly old, wooden sailing ships—and the bones of crew who left port and didn't make it back. There was no question in my mind in October that Walbridge should have anticipated problems with Sandy and that *Bounty* should have remained at some dock, some place, and should not have ventured out toward an approaching hurricane.

I was grateful, then, when Mike offered me the opportunity to investigate *Bounty*'s saga and ask what to me was the critical question: Why did Robin Walbridge take his ship to sea?

In March 2013, I climbed over a snow bank in Quincy, Massachusetts, and knocked on the door of a house where Robin Walbridge's maternal grandparents had lived.

Lucille Walbridge Jansen came to the door and listened while I explained that I would like to talk with her about her brother. She was grieving the loss of the boy she grew up calling Robert. But she graciously welcomed me inside and, for an hour, listened as I attempted to convince her that she should share her memories. Then she asked me a simple question: How is your book going to be different from all the others?

I told Mrs. Jansen that Mike and I would write the most comprehensive and accurate story, one that attempted to answer all the questions. She agreed that I could visit in two weeks.

The stories that she began to tell in that next visit painted a picture of Robert/Robin that transformed him from being a caricature into a real person with unique qualities, passions, and abilities. Her tales helped show me why her brother could be adored by so many, respected by almost all he met. They also gave shape to an intelligent, driven man who, in the end, was trapped by his own success, almost universally unquestioned and, perhaps as a result, unaccustomed to being challenged.

Above anyone else whom I have encountered working on this book, then, I owe a debt of gratitude and affection to Lucille Walbridge Jansen and her husband, Peter Jansen.

I hope that in repayment of that debt, our work will provide readers with an honest portrait of a man whose enthusiasm for his life touched many, often young, people and no doubt changed in a positive way the course of their lives.

ACKNOWLEDGMENTS

The authors wish to thank all the people we either interviewed or corresponded with. You were gracious with your time and opened up your hearts.

ABOUT THE AUTHORS

DOUGLAS A. CAMPBELL

Doug Campbell is the author of two nonfiction books for adults: *The Sea's Bitter Harvest* and *Eight Survived*. He has spent his career in journalism. For twenty-five years, he was a staff writer at the *Philadelphia Inquirer*, where two of his stories were nominated for the Pulitzer Prize. Later he won numerous awards as a senior writer at *Soundings* magazine, covering all aspects of recreational boating. Doug began sailing on the Delaware River in 1979 and still keeps a small boat moored there. He and his wife, Monica, also sail a thirty-two-foot blue water boat, *Robin*, with which they've competed in the biennial Bermuda One-Two Yacht Race. Doug has placed third out of thirty-nine boats on corrected time sailing the single-handed leg of the race from Newport, Rhode Island, to Bermuda.

MICHAEL J. TOUGIAS

New York Times–bestselling author Michael Tougias has earned critical acclaim, literary awards, and legions of fans for his bestselling nonfiction narratives. Many of his thirty-six books have a predominant theme of true survival-at-sea adventures. His stories honor real-life, everyday people who rise to face life-threatening situations, make heroic choices, and survive against the odds. Tougias frequently speaks at schools, libraries, and to groups of all sizes. He lives in Massachusetts and Florida.

www.michaeltougias.com

Middle Reader Books Authored and Co-Authored by Michael J. Tougias

Tougias and Henry Holt & Company have released several books in their True Rescue series.

The Finest Hours was chosen as a Junior Library Guild selection, a Scholastic selection, an Amazon Best Book of the Month, and a Children's Book Council selection. The middle reader version of *The Finest Hours* landed at #3 on the *New York Times* Children's Bestseller List.

A Storm Too Soon was also a Junior Library Guild selection, a Barnes & Noble Top Pick for Kids, and a Scholastic selection. In addition, it was also a National Council of Social Studies Notable book, a selection from Texas Library Association Topaz Reading List, and a finalist for Cybils Literary Award. *Kirkus* praised the book, saying "Tougias's urgent present-tense narration places readers in the action with smoothly woven detours adding fascinating details. A sure-fire hit with young readers." *VOYA* enthused, "Tougias provides crisp, clean prose for his young readers. As the storm surges so does the author's prose."

INTO THE BLIZZARD: HEROISM AT SEA DURING THE GREAT BLIZZARD OF 1978

- A Scholastic selection

- *Kirkus Reviews*: "Reads like a thriller. Riveting."

- Amazon Book of the Month

- A Junior Library Guild selection

ATTACKED AT SEA: A TRUE WORLD WAR II STORY OF A FAMILY'S FIGHT FOR SURVIVAL

- A Scholastic selection

- Amazon Book of the Month

- A Junior Library Guild selection

IN HARM'S WAY: THE SINKING OF THE USS *INDIANAPOLIS* AND THE EXTRAORDINARY STORY OF ITS SURVIVORS

Tougias's other books for Young Adults & Middle Readers

- *The Cringe Chronicles: Mortifying Misadventures with My Dad* (coauthored by Kristin Tougias)

- *Claws*

- *Until I Have No Country: A Novel of King Philip's War*

- *Derek's Gift: A True Story of Love, Courage and Lessons Learned*